THE BUSINESS STRATEGY OF SUCCESS

ROBERTO SERVITJE

THE BUSINESS STRATEGY OF SUCCESS

OCÉANO

BIMBO
The Business Strategy of Success

Original title: BIMBO. Estrategia de éxito empresarial

© 2024, Roberto Servitje Sendra

Translation: Alicia Morales / Leticia Marín

Cover design: Ivonne Murillo
Photograph of Roberto Servitje: courtesy of the author

D. R. © 2025, Editorial Océano de México, S.A. de C.V.
Guillermo Barroso 17-5, Col. Industrial Las Armas
Tlalnepantla de Baz, 54080, Estado de México
info@oceano.com.mx

First edition in English: 2025

ISBN: 978-607-557-964-1

No part of this publication may be reproduced stored in a retrieval system or transmitted in any form, or by any means (electronic, mechanical, or otherwise) without the prior written permission of both the copyright owners and the Publisher.

Printed in Mexico

Contents

Acknowledgements 15
Introduction 17
About the author 19
Foreword 25
A preliminary message from the author 27

CHAPTER 1. THE ORIGIN OF GRUPO BIMBO 29
The founders 29
- Some background 30

Internationalization 35
The birth of a winner 41

CHAPTER 2. FACTORS THAT FOSTERED OUR GROWTH 43
The value of effort 43
- Our trust in Mexico 43

Integration 44
- Our desire to grow. Territorial expansion 45

Reinvestment 46
Maintenance of quality, austerity and service policies 46
- Line Diversification 47
- Delegation 47

Exporting/internationalization 47
Order, cleanliness and quality 47

Modernization—State-of-the-art-technology 48
The structure 50
Summary of Grupo Bimbo's secrets for success 50
Our contribution to the consumer 53

CHAPTER 3. OUR BACKBONE 55
The importance of a company philosophy 55
The company as institution, its inclusion in history 60
Economic systems 61
- Subsistence economy 61
- Planned, authoritarian and centralized economy 61
- Market or free market economy 62

Towards a socially responsible company 62

CHAPTER 4. PHILOSOPHY OF THE COMPANY 67
A company with high values and principles 67
Personality 67
Excellence 68
Being more 68
- Ideals and objectives 69
- Inner peace 69

The price of success 70
Social Assembly of Mexican Entrepreneurs 71
Core principles and beliefs 72
- Integrity 73
- The dignity of the person 76
- Solidarity: sharing versus competing 77

Worrying or taking action 79
Subsidiarity 80
Happiness 80
The value of work 81

Great thinkers and management concepts 83
- Peter Drucker 83
- Charles McCormick 84
- Rensis Likert 84
- Douglas McGregor 84
- Lincoln Electric 85
- Carlos Llano 85
- Shigeru Kobayashi 86
- Scott Myers 86
- Tanner and Athos 88
- Sergio Reyes 89
- Tom Peters and Roberto H. Waterman 89
- Philip Crosby 91
- Kaoru Ishikawa, Joseph Juran and Edwards Deming 92
- Jack Welch 93

CHAPTER 5. TOWARDS A TRANSFORMATION OF THE COMPANY 95
The need for transformation 95
Problems are opportunities 99
Through participation 100

CHAPTER 6. HOW TO MAKE PROGRESS IN PARTICIPATION 103
Participation in information 105
Participation in consultation 107
Functional participation 108
- Empowerment 111

Profit participation 111
Ownership participation 113
Institutional participation 118

CHAPTER 7. A MISSION AND AN IDEAL 121

To serve, our reasen for being 121
Our mission 122
Our ideal 124
Shaping a culture 125
Our beliefs 131
- We Value the Person 134
- We are One Community 134
- We Compete and Win 134
- We Act with Integrity 134
- We Get Results 134
- We are Sharp Operators 135
- We Transcend and Endure 135

Our vision 135
Our Code of Ethics. Background 135
- Bribes at customs 136
- Road traffic violations 137
- Relations with labor unions 137
- Removing surplus personnel 137
- My retirement as CEO 139
- Hiring and permanence of vice presidents 139

Our Code of Ethics 140
- Towards consumers and customers 140
- Towards shareholders and partners 140
- Towards associates 141
- Towards suppliers 141
- Towards society 141
- Towards our competitors 142
- In our day-to-day operation 142
- Assets protection 142
- Compliance with legislation 142
- Commitment of the leaders 143

CHAPTER 8. A COMPANY WILL BE WHAT ITS PERSONNEL ARE, AND ITS PERSONNEL WILL BE WHAT THEIR LEADERS ARE 145

In Bimbo we offer jobs, not gigs 145
- In games and in reality 146

Developing our personnel's trust 147
- Beijing 147

Guidelines 149
Other stimulating traits 152
The leaders' policies 154
Leadership 155
Nature of leadership 158
Characteristics of a leader 161

CHAPTER 9. CHALLENGES 167

Productivity 167
- *Apparent* work 168
- Reasonable productivity 169

Productivity and austerity 169
- Productivity, the engine of modern life 170
- Personal productivity 172

Productivity in a global economy 175
Globalization 179
- How we insert ourselves into globalization 180

Points to consider regarding internationalization 181
- Market research 181
- The government 182
- Customs, mores and culture 182

What we can learn from globalization 182
- Conclusions about our responsibility as entrepreneurs given globalization 185

Outstanding challenges for Grupo Bimbo 185

Outstanding challenges for Developing
and Third World countries 186

CHAPTER 10. SOME PERSONAL IDEAS 187
The country that we want 187
The vote 187
To unite or to separate 193

APPENDIX 1. CHRONOLOGY OF BAKERIES AND PLANTS 195

APPENDIX 2. TOTAL QUALITY AND REENGINEERING 207
Total quality. A general perspective 209
- First stage. Making contact 209
  - *The beginning of change* 210
- Second stage 210
  - *Corporate projects* 211
- Third stage. Support aspects 213
- Fourth stage. Consolidation 214
- Bimbo quality model 214
  - *Definition of processes* 215
  - *Starting the projects* 215
- How do Continuous Improvement and
  Reengineering supplement each other? 218

Epilogue 221

Final note 223

MY MOTHER

I wish to dedicate this work, albeit briefly, to my mother, Josefina Sendra de Servitje. Mrs. Pepita, as lovingly addressed by family, friends and associates.

She was born in a small town in Barcelona, Spain, the sixth of nine children. She studied very little since her father's premature death meant she had to work to help at home. When she was 23 years old, she arrived in Mexico, where she married my father, Juan Servitje Torrallardona, who also died very young. Upon his death, my mother, who was only 44 years old, had to take care of us, who were quite young, and of the two-family businesses.

She was always an example of strength and hard work, with an indomitable iron will. Growing up, I believed it was natural for people to work and make a massive effort like she did, and she taught us to do the same. I soon discovered that she was exceptional.

From my mother, a physically and spiritually strong woman, we learned, almost inadvertently, to work with absolute dedication and perseverance. We learned to be austere and frugal, and in the end, she left us a precious legacy of Christian faith and personal integrity.

TININA

I also want to dedicate this book to my wonderful wife since I would not have succeeded without her support, encouragement, patience and understanding. We got married very young with great hopes, but we faced shortages, enormous work pressures, travel, absences, and a lot of moving.

Although back then, that was apparently what we had to do, she undoubtedly got the short end of the stick, which demanded all her generosity and selflessness.

It would only be fair to talk about my achievements if I acknowledged the fundamental role that my wife played in them.

Acknowledgements

I wish to express my sincere gratitude to the people who encouraged me to write this book.

First, to my brother Lorenzo because his concepts and example helped shape my convictions.

To the Unión Social de Empresarios de México (USEM) [Social Union of Mexico's Entrepreneurs], for it was there that for four decades, I have received light and encouragement in matters of Social Doctrine.

To my wife Tinina for her understanding, her love, and the inspiration she has brought into my life. To my children, whom I love dearly.

To Gardina Soria, my secretary of many years, who classified and organized my writings.

To Javier Millán[†] for his support in revising and organizing the original manuscript. I am particularly grateful to Víctor Milke[†], who was incredibly dedicated to helping me rearrange this new edition.

And, of course, to all my co-workers, those who are no longer with us and those who continue working in the bakeries, the sales centers, and our Group's Offices in Mexico and abroad. Their collaboration, dedication and example have made our highest aspirations a reality.

Introduction

I am convinced that the happiness we desire may only be attained if we succeed in being good parents, entrepreneurs, and citizens, set our ideals based on great beliefs and sound principles, and are honest and uphold a clear sense of service.

Today, with over 80 years of experience, I do not believe a rising career can be built without a good measure of hard work. In my opinion, those seeking to achieve energetic, meritorious progress will not enjoy a forty-five-hour work week.

Many years ago, when someone asked if we worked five-day weeks, we always said no; we told them we worked more than 80 hours per week; of course, nowadays, this is no longer necessary, although some managers with big ambitions work longer days than usual, of their own volition, to attain their goals.

After more than 25 years in Grupo Bimbo's Corporate Office, I still remember working in the bakery, which, although demanding, was a gratifying experience. In management, we plan, control, and make tough decisions, but we always long for and need contact with the actual operation and the people working the line.

Roberto Servitje Sendra

Don Roberto, as Bimbo's associates affectionately refer to him, was CEO of the company from 1978 to 1997 and President of the Board of Directors from 1994 to 2013.

About the author

Roberto Servitje Sendra, born in 1928 in Mexico City and former Chairman of Grupo Bimbo's Board of Directors, has always abided by his core values, among many others: consideration of all people as human beings and the search for quality, productivity, and austerity.

The son of Catalan immigrants, founders of the famous El Molino pastry shop (which, incidentally, was the first link in the chain that would become the powerful group he presided over since 1994), Roberto completed his initial studies in Mexico City. He then studied Humanities at the Jean de Brebeuf School, led by Jesuit priests, in Montreal, Canada (1943-1945). During his stay in that country, he was a member of the Aviation Cadets of the Royal Canadian Air Force (RCAF).

Upon his return from Canada, he enrolled in the Escuela Bancaria y Comercial (Banking and Commercial School) of Mexico City, where he studied Accounting. Immediately, he started working in a pharmaceutical business and then moved on to the Servitje y Mata company. On September 17, 1945, at seventeen, he started working at Bimbo. He began as a sales supervisor and later created the vehicle department.

His career as a businessman began in 1956 when he founded Bimbo de Occidente in Guadalajara and served as its General Manager. He was responsible for opening markets and commercial development in several states, setting up the bakery in that year, and commercial development that led him to cover half of the Mexican territory in just under five years.

Later, he moved to Monterrey, where he waged a fierce battle against the competition. When the conflict was solved, he returned to Mexico City as the General Manager of Panificación Bimbo. He held that position for six years.

In 1969, he traveled to Boston, where he graduated from the Program for Management Development (PMD) at Harvard University. He then returned to assume the position of Deputy Director of Organización Bimbo, which he would hold for nine years. By 1978, the Organization already had 13 bakeries.

In 1979, he was appointed CEO of Grupo Bimbo, and eleven years later, he became the Company's Executive Chair. The Group grew significantly during that time: 24 operating companies were created, totaling 50. In 1994, he was appointed Chairman of the Board of Directors and President of the Group.

He was a founding member of the Company and its first associate. Among his most noteworthy contributions to the business, the following come to mind: intense, quality-centered work and technological innovation, an unwavering pursuit of productivity, which he likes to call "the infinite possibility," and a ceaseless effort to create a more humane and participatory company, which he achieved, mainly due to his discipline and his habit of continuously visiting the plants.

In June of 1995, Lorenzo Servitje, founder of Grupo Bimbo, stated the following regarding Roberto, his younger brother:

> I wish to highlight that the last 15 years of Bimbo are Roberto's significant contribution to the Group, especially regarding innovation and the Group's dynamics. Roberto has found a way to achieve balance in our philosophy, making Bimbo a highly productive and, at the same time, a deeply humane company.

Roberto Servitje has carried out other academic and social-oriented activities. He has taught at the Instituto Panamericano de Alta Dirección de Empresas (IPADE) [Panamerican Institute for Top Management] and in Cursos de Formación Social (CUFOSO) [Course for Social Education]. He was President of USEM-Mexico and Chairman of the Confederación USEM, affiliate to

UNIAPAC, with its main offices in Brussels, from 1984 to 1987. He has given conferences, among which the following should be highlighted: in Mexico, he has spoken at the Unión Social de Empresarios de México (USEM) [Social Union of Mexico's Entrepreneurs], at the Instituto Tecnológico y de Estudios Superiores de Monterrey (ITESM) [Technological Institute and for High Education of Monterrey], in the Instituto Tecnológico Autónomo de México (ITAM) [Autonomous Technological Institute of Mexico], at the Konrad Adenauer Foundation and the Iberoamericana, De las Américas, Bonaterra, Panamericana and Anáhuac Universities. Abroad, Roberto has spoken at the Business Schools of Harvard and Northwestern Universities, at McGill University in Montreal, Canada, at Darden University in Virginia, at the Instituto de Estudios Superiores de la Empresa (IESE) [Enterprise High Education Institute] of the University of Navarra in Barcelona and the IUVE Foundation in Madrid. In Grupo Bimbo, he is a speaker in the Curso del Líder (Leadership Seminar) and in the Be a Better You Course (BBY) [Curso de Superación Personal (CUSUPE in Spanish)], where his talk The Ideal is unfailingly deemed outstanding. As a Board Member, he has collaborated with various banks, companies, and institutions.

In 1988, the Confederación Mexicana de Ejecutivos de Ventas y Mercadotecnia, A.C. named him *Executive of the Year*. In 2002, La Salle Noroeste University awarded him the degree of *Doctor Honoris Causa*. In 2007, he and his brother Lorenzo were inducted into the Baking Hall of Fame of the American Society of Baking.

Roberto Servitje married Yolanda Achútegui. They have five children, 21 grandchildren and 42 great-grandchildren. He is a tireless traveler and a student of several languages. Among his interests are aviation, painting, mechanics, reading, writing, and computer sciences.

In 2015, he was granted the *"Pro Ecclesia et Pontifice"* medal by Pope Francis.

Roberto Servitje Sendra, as described by his wife

In Roberto, I have found a faithful and loving life companion, an admirable husband, strict and with unbending morals yet understanding and generous. He has been the guide, the example, and the pillar from whom all family members seek support.

He is a virtuous man who, first and foremost, loves God, his fellow people, his family, and his work. A man who supports his valuable advice and teachings by example. He treasures and knows how to enjoy family life.

His social interests have been translated into a concern for creating new sources of employment, becoming increasingly productive, and striving to have his social principles practiced and increasingly disseminated.

Roberto is a multifaceted person. His great aptitude for languages and music and many skills make him suitable for countless other pursuits.

He always finishes what he starts, never leaving things halfway; he constantly thinks about creating new things and doing more.

Roberto Servitje, as seen by his son

My father has always been a man of firm Christian convictions, an iron will and deep love for everyone around him; he is the object of pride not only of his offspring but also of many other people who have met him.

He has been a loving father who taught us to love God and keep Him in the center of our lives, even before he taught us how to walk; through his example, he instilled in us the values of responsibility, fairness, honesty, and commitment to others.

The most important legacy my father ever gave me was "wings" to soar and become what I want to be.

Roberto Servitje, from the perspective of his grandson

My grandfather is deeply admired, not only by his family but by many people. He is a hard-working man, always ready to solve any problem he might face. He is devoted to his family, his work and God. He invariably fulfills his responsibilities, measuring the consequences of his actions. My grandfather takes his personal life and contact with his associates very seriously.

He is a man with strong moral and spiritual values who is always willing to help others. We have always loved him for his kindness and desire to share his life and joy with us.

Thank you, grandfather!

Foreword

Personal and corporate success depend on diverse factors, but for it to endure, success must be based on sound values and principles. This is the message issued by Roberto Servitje Sendra, one of the most successful Mexican business leaders of our time. As he points out in his book, "Only the companies which attain institutional strength through a solid moral base, with a firm set of guiding principles, will prevail."

It is an important message we must all heed, particularly when constant change has accelerated exponentially with new technologies, bringing the world into globalization. The speed of transformation in all areas and the availability of such an extraordinary amount of information demand that companies respond instantly to the ever-changing needs of consumers and market conditions. In today's world, successful companies no longer stand out merely due to what they know but also for the speed with which they make decisions based on their knowledge and ability to generate savings, improve efficiency, learn, and constantly fine-tune their production and service rendering processes. In this context, companies require a solid foundation to guide their strategic development, enabling them to overcome the multiple challenges entailed by such an extremely volatile environment. A well-defined corporate philosophy and the highest values and principles provide that foundation.

It is difficult not to deviate from those principles and values when short-term economic pressures arise. The case of Grupo Bimbo is a perfect example.

Its Company's philosophy is summarized in two words: *believe* and *create*.

Believe, first and foremost, in people; people *as an end and not as a means* to achieving full corporate and human growth, where planned goals may only be attained through the collaboration and commitment of all those who make up a company.

Believe in integrity, not only as a business practice that yields great profit but also as a social responsibility that must be fully embraced for the company to overcome challenges as complex as corruption, thus contributing to any country's economic, social, and cultural progress. Finally, believe in the fundamental importance of leadership to generate a sense of mission, instill a genuine, service-oriented attitude, and fulfill commitments to society.

This philosophy, in turn, rests on a series of fundamental values such as honesty, justice, and equity, which, in the corporate thinking of Roberto Servitje, regulate human relations inside and outside a company in dealing with consumers, customers, suppliers, authorities and society. A company's management must explicitly represent such values in its code of ethics to ensure all of its members share and apply them consistently in their national and international operations, as this is the only way in which they will help the company consolidate this projection. Throughout this book, we will learn how Grupo Bimbo became one of the most successful Mexican companies, one of the most widely acknowledged and prestigious brands, and an essential part of an entire culture based on a straightforward corporate philosophy and its shared values.

In this book, Roberto Servitje allows us to understand better his thinking, strategic vision, high sense of responsibility, and passion for Mexico. It becomes crystal clear that one of the main characteristics of an authentic leader is his ability to communicate.

Lorenzo H. Zambrano Treviño
Chairman of the Board and CEO of CEMEX,
1985–2014

A preliminary message from the author

Some time ago, a dear friend invited me to write this book. I thanked him for his kind suggestion but answered I did not want to do it back then. I believed the market was full of books about the right path in the world of business and that more were being published each day. It seemed pretentious of me to believe there could be an interest in what I could write.

Nonetheless, I agreed to do it sometime later, nudged by new insistence and new arguments. Why? I finally understood that it could be a way to lend continuity to the effort I have carried out for decades with hope and enthusiasm.

Indeed, I have dedicated many hours of my life to conveying to my business colleagues and young people who aspire to begin their careers my deep conviction that corporations play a decisive role in the behavior of society and, therefore, they must respond to what society expects from them. The company is, without a doubt, the driver of the socioeconomic life of a country, and as such, it shapes its inhabitants' lifestyles. Peter Drucker, an admired and respected management specialist, stated: "Inasmuch as the problems of businesses are solved, the problems of society will be solved."

Given the fundamental role that the company plays in the social environment, we must acknowledge that it has the enormous responsibility of fulfilling its economic objectives and achieving its social purposes and that all of us, as its leaders, must live up to such a high responsibility.

Now, more than ever, the company must respond to society's desires by being effective, efficient, profitable, creative, responsible, and completely ethical.

Traditionally, companies have dedicated themselves to the service of a few; however, our present reality demands that they be at the service of all, that they be entities with a soul, which will not only allow but promote the fulfillment of all their members and the common good.

A firm conviction regarding the company's importance and transcendence and the imperative need for its leaders to be prepared to carry out the transformations it might require has been a standard in my performance; at the same time, it has been an incentive to share the disciplines and values that may lay the foundations for such an evolution.

This is why I decided to write this book: to convey my concerns to a larger number of people more permanently through its pages.

With the best intentions, I express concepts and convey experiences of many years that may enrich corporate life and foster a fairer, more humane society.

Chapter 1
The Origin of Grupo Bimbo

Sometimes, people ask me if any of the founders of Grupo Bimbo ever imagined we would be present in so many places around the country and abroad. The truth is, we never imagined it.

In the inauguration document of Panificación Bimbo, on December 2, 1945, there are two words that I consider to be the answer to the question: *Believe-Create.*

For me, the foundations of this great company were faith in God and visualizing the value of work as an extension of His creative work.

Our beloved Group, throughout the years, became a reality through the tens of thousands of people who contributed with their daily, intense, and enthusiastic work and their constant concern for quality, customer service and productivity.

Just as a grain of wheat multiplies, the seeds that each of our associates, shareholders, suppliers, and customers has planted with faith and affection have multiplied, and to all of them, after God, we owe our place today.

This is why I wish to start this book by saying *thank you* and renewing the hope in *Believe* and *Create*.

THE FOUNDERS

Grupo Bimbo was founded with Mexican equity in 1944. Lorenzo, my older brother, who was 28 years old, played an essential role from the start. Many contributed with ideas, but when he said *yes and in this way*, he endowed the company with its spirit and style from the beginning. In addition to my brother Lorenzo, other people participated in the company's foundation, including José Mata (one of Lorenzo's schoolmates), Jaime Jorba (our brother-in-law), Alfonso Velasco (a man of great and varied abilities) and, on a smaller scale, Jaime Sendra (our uncle), and I. Even though I cannot grant Lorenzo full merit for the creation of the Group, I can say that he was its main driving force.

Some background

The first European settlers to arrive in America introduced the loaf of bread. Later, its name was changed to Pullman Bread because it was served in railroad restaurant cars called Pullman.

In Mexico, this sort of bread was offered first for internal consumption in the Sylvain restaurant at the beginning of the 20th century.

During the 1920s, Mr. Martín Velasco established a small bakery to produce loaves of bread in Mexico, and he sent his son Alfonso to study a technical course on breadmaking at the American Institute of Baking in the USA.

The company went bankrupt when it faced a severe economic crisis. Still, it was rebuilt as Pan Ideal in 1926 with new owners, who also started the bakery Ideal, where my father, Don Juan Servitje, started working.

My father was of Catalan background, as was my mother, Mrs. Josefina Sendra. Two years later, my father decided to break away from the Ideal bakery and established his own, supported by my mother, an enterprising woman with great initiative.

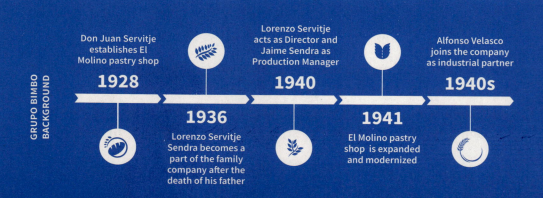

And this was how, in 1928, the El Molino pastry shop came into existence.

In 1936, when my brother Lorenzo was 18 years old, our father died, so Lorenzo had to quit his formal education to help our mother manage the family business.

At that time, Alfonso Velasco, son of Martín Velasco, worked as Technical Director at Pan Ideal. Alfonso's knowledge ranged from baking all types of bread to making sweet baked goods and cakes, and his expertise in managing and maintaining the most complex industrial machinery made him the most prominent technician in this field in Mexico.

Back then, Pan Ideal's quality and service were quite deficient in adequately satisfying the growing demand for this product, perhaps because it faced no competition.

By then, young Lorenzo was already the El Molino pastry shop manager, and his uncle, Mr. Jaime Sendra, was head of production.

In 1941, El Molino pastry shop expanded and became the largest and most modern bakery in Mexico City. Mr. Alfonso Velasco, then technical director of Pan Ideal, was invited to install new ovens.

Later, when the management of El Molino decided to make loaves of bread to sell wholesale throughout the city, thus venturing into the branch of industrial bakeries, they invited Alfonso Velasco to become an industrial partner, as he already had vast experience in this field. He enthusiastically accepted. His ideas to improve the business, packaging, products, and distribution proved priceless in establishing and developing this new company.

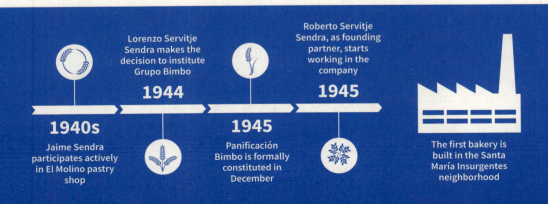

Jaime Jorba, my cousin, worked for some time at the El Molino pastry shop. Years later, he married Miss Josefina Servitje Sendra, our sister. With an innate talent for sales, great vitality and drive, and a spirited sense of humor, Jaime was a crucial factor in the company's development that was beginning to take shape. So, he became another one of the pillars for Bimbo's success.

The growing market, which demanded better service and higher-quality, fresher bread, was an opportunity that the founders of Panificación Bimbo took advantage of to turn the company into the undisputed leader of bread loaves in Mexico.

Participating in the foundation of Grupo Bimbo represented a true challenge for me, as I was very young. I had just returned from studying in Canada. I was studying at the Escuela Bancaria y Comercial in the evenings when my brother Lorenzo invited me to invest in the company, warning me that I would have to "give this job my best." I accepted his proposal and even started working at Bimbo before him on September 17, 1945, whereas Lorenzo began in December that same year. In fact, I got there so early that the building was still under construction. My brother continued as manager of El Molino, and I was already working in sales at Grupo Bimbo. The other supervisor and I visited our customers all over Mexico City on foot, creating routes to investigate whether there was acceptance for specific products. When I started working, Mr. Velasco, who had a unique personality, knowledge and various abilities that made him a wonderful character, had already begun installing the new equipment.

The first bakery was built in the Santa María Insurgentes neighborhood on one-third of a 10,000-square-meter plot sold to us by Mr. Daniel Montull, Lorenzo's father-in-law. Two years later, the company had grown so much that the existing facilities had to be enlarged, and an additional third of the land was used; four years later, the whole plot housed the bakery.

Those first facilities are still there, although they do not look as they did when the original bakery was built.

The Origin of Grupo Bimbo

In June of 2024, Grupo Bimbo:

- has over 220 bakeries, other plants, and trading companies in 35 countries around the world, with over 100 brands, making it the largest baking company in the world;
- has over 152,000 associates;
- reached 22.5 billion dollars in sales in 2023, and
- has been listed on the Mexican Stock Exchange since 1980.

Countries where Grupo Bimbo is present

Argentina	France	Panama	Switzerland
Brazil	Guatemala	Paraguay	Tunisia
Canada	Honduras	Peru	Turkey
Chile	India	Portugal	Ukraine
China	Italy	Romania	United Kingdom
Colombia	Kazakhstan	Russia	United States of America
Costa Rica	Mexico	South Africa	Uruguay
Ecuador	Morocco	South Korea	Venezuela
El Salvador	Nicaragua	Spain	

Some of its leading brands are:

Oroweat	Marinela
Thomas'	Entenmann's
Barcel	Bimbo
Sara Lee	

Its main categories are:

Sliced bread	Salty snacks
Pastries	Bagels
Buns & rolls	English muffins
Toast	Tortillas & flatbreads
Cakes	Cookies

As integration activities—activities not core to the business but that intrinsically conform to or shape the products—the Group had specialized machinery production companies. It also participates in other small businesses that supply different products. These associations have been consolidated to ensure the quality and consistency required to work with reliable processes.

Starting in 2000, Grupo Bimbo made the significant decision to divest from the six flour mills that supplied 75 percent of its raw materials and from two fruit and vegetable processing plants that produced jams and fillings. This decision was made to appease the concern of the Group's senior management to focus on their core activities by avoiding the diversion of funds and attention to aspects that, albeit strategic, do not belong to their fundamental field; this turned out to be a decision that was undoubtedly correct. In 2022, Grupo Bimbo signed an agreement with Mondelēz International to sell its confectionery business, which included the brands Ricolino, Vero, La Corona and Coronado, among others.

INTERNATIONALIZATION

In the international field, Grupo Bimbo's experience began 19 years after its creation. In 1963, Mr. Jaime Jorba, one of our founding partners, decided to return to Spain to establish a bakery under the Bimbo brand. It opened in Barcelona and was so successful that another one was opened shortly after in Madrid. Five bakeries were operating in that country by the beginning of the seventies.

For different reasons, but mainly because Grupo Bimbo in Mexico didn't want to invest resources abroad, the Spanish group gradually became a majority. At that time, strong leftist unrest stirred the country, and relations with the bakeries' personnel became difficult, leading many partners to sell their stock to an American company. Sometime later, we had some differences with the new partners, and we ended up selling all our shares to them.

In 1969, we decided to venture into other countries; we did not plan to set up bakeries abroad but rather to export. Where to? I remember a somewhat funny anecdote that Emilio Azcárraga Milmo[†] (former Chief Executive Officer of Televisa, a Mexican telecommunications and broadcasting company) used to tell. He said that when he thought of going abroad to grow the company, he told his father he was thinking of starting by going to Guatemala, El Salvador and that entire area, and his father told him: "Don't be such a … if you want to reach out, go North, not South." So, I told myself:

FIRST MILESTONE IN THE INTERNATIONALIZATION OF GRUPO BIMBO

1964: the first bakery with the Bimbo brand is founded in Barcelona.

Beginning of the decade of 1970: five bakeries operate in the Iberian Peninsula.

"We're going to go up; we're not going to start below," so we started trying to export to the United States. We failed several times, as we didn't have the total quality mentality we have now; often, our products did not fulfill their standards and were returned to us. The same thing happened with the fruit ships we exported to Europe.

We are talking about a time almost 50 years ago when these failures pushed us to work hard until we reached the total quality mentality.

As the United States was undoubtedly an area of great importance for our development, after several unsuccessful attempts to export into this country, in 1984, we established two small distributors of our products: one in Texas, based in Houston, and another in Los Angeles, California.

Over the years, these companies grew until they became actual instruments of introduction, reaching nearby markets and cities as far away as Chicago and Miami.

The next step was to explore the market for wheat and corn tortillas. To this end, we gradually acquired small Mexican-owned bakeries in California, Texas, Oklahoma, and Ohio.

As expected, opportunities to acquire bakeries arose, so we bought some in San Diego and Los Angeles, where we later purchased the bakery Four-S-Webber. However, the most important acquisition was that of Mrs. Baird's Group, a century-old family business with ten bakeries in Texas.

When we carried out this operation, we noticed that, from the administrative point of view, the situation was complicated, and consolidation was necessary; thus, in 1999, the American company Bimbo Bakeries USA was created, covering all our companies in that country. For the same reason, a corporate office was created in Fort Worth to manage all the operations and report them to the Headquarters in Mexico. At the beginning of 2002, the most important acquisition that the Group had ever made took place: the purchase of five bakeries and the manufacturing rights of the Premium line of bread in the United States. From the company George Weston Bakeries, we acquired their operation on the Pacific Coast, encompassing the following brands: Oroweat, Entenmann's, Thomas', and Boboli. We believe the latter has been a strategic purchase of great importance for the Group since it consolidated our operations in that important country, which now spans its entire territory.

At the end of 2023, sales in North America, including the United States and Canada, accounted for 48.1% of the company's 22.5 billion dollars, i.e., 10.823 billion dollars.

So far, we have had numerous experiences on the American continent, both in the South and the North, and we have strived to take advantage of the opportunities presented to us through immediate synergies or long-term strategies.

The next goal was to grow towards the South, which was simplified for us when, in 1990, we advised a small cake manufacturing company in Guatemala. The company later invited us to participate as partners due to its lack of capital. After some time, we remodeled their bakery and started producing a line of products under the Bimbo and Marinela brands.

The following country we went to in the South, in 1992, was Chile, where we were offered the chance to partner with two companies, one manufacturing loaves of bread (Ideal) and the other a producer of salty snacks (Alesa). They even sent us pictures and a detailed report on these companies. Initially, we thought: "No way, why would we want to go to Chile?" But one of our top managers insisted, and we sent our people to scout the land until we finally decided to accept the partnership. After a few years, we had to shut down the old, deficient facilities with which we had started and built a modern bread loaf bakery, and since our partners no longer wanted to invest, the partnership was dissolved. The Ministries of Foreign Affairs and Commerce of Chile helped us so we could operate under the Bimbo brand; in the end, we could not do so because a cookie company had already registered the brand for one of its products. So, we went on with the brand Ideal, which we had acquired initially, but we gave it the Bimbo image, with the bear, the colors and all its distinctive features. Later, we decided not to continue marketing salty snacks in South America and sold that company.

In 1993, we arrived in Venezuela, where the Polar company offered us a bakery where we could produce our products, which it had acquired years

Bimbo. A Strategy for Corporate Success

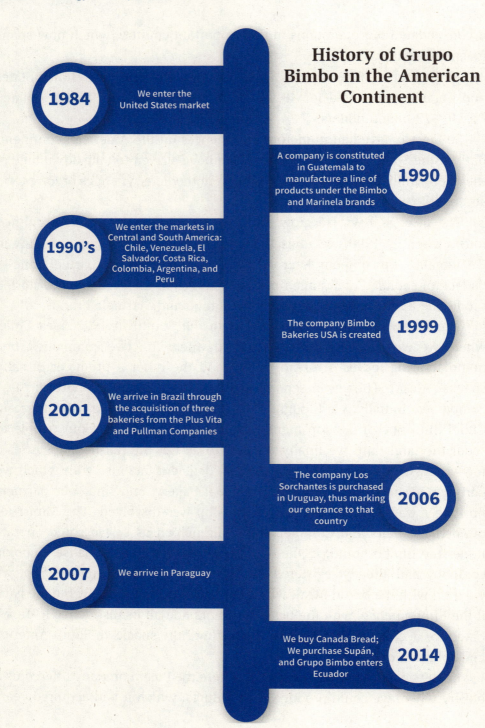

before. It was large and modern, but its location could have been better; however, it seemed like an excellent opportunity to enter that country, so we acquired and remodeled it. Sometime later, they offered to sell us Panificadora Holsum, Venezuela's most important bread loaf producer. Our experience in that geography had not been very successful due to variations and the political and economic volatility in the country.

That same year, we were able to enter San Salvador, as the bread manufacturer Las Victorias offered to sell us their small bakery. Since we did not have a bread production line in Guatemala, we decided to combine both operations and work out some synergy, so we decided to go ahead with the acquisition. Over time, we have expanded and adapted this bakery, mainly serving the Central American market.

Years later, we made inroads in Costa Rica, where we acquired the bakery Cinta Azul. After some expansions and revamping, we turned it into Bimbo. We recently added another line of baking specialties and the Breddy line to this operation.

We went on to Colombia, where, in 1996, associated with Grupo Noel from Medellín (Union of Antioquia), we inaugurated a new Bimbo bakery in Bogotá.

In 1997, we landed in Argentina. Negotiations with local manufacturers were unsuccessful, so we built a beautiful and modern bakery on our own, perhaps the most advanced of the Group at that time regarding technology (President Menem congratulated us profusely when he inaugurated it). Without a doubt, our experience in Argentina has been the most challenging and costly, as we have yet to reach our sales goals. The bread lines have yielded good results, but the same has yet to happen with the other lines. Despite everything, we have gradually been moving forward. However, there is little certainty about what may happen due to the ambiguous situation prevailing in that country.

In 1998, we entered Lima, Peru, by invitation of Alicorp Corporate Group, with which we partnered to establish a Bimbo bakery. We went into business with them, aware that this was a small market with an economy undergoing a transformation; therefore, we do not expect short-term positive results; rather, we deem it a good strategy to introduce our brands in Latin America in the near future. We arrived in Brazil at the beginning of 2001 by acquiring three Plus Vita company bakeries, one in Sao Paulo, one in Rio and another in Recife. These bakeries constitute a new challenge that will enable us to be present practically in all of South America, including Uruguay, Panama, and Paraguay, where later on, we bought a competing company, Nutrella, which has, in turn, made it possible for us to consolidate our presence and coverage in that country.

From the bakeries mentioned above, we supply other countries in the region, such as Honduras and Nicaragua, where we are studying the possibility of installing production plants in the future.

We moved from South America to the East, where, in 2006, we acquired our first bakery in Beijing, the capital of China.

As the reader may see, in all cases, we have tried to partner with companies or people from the countries in question. The experiences in this sense have been diverse: we have minority shareholders in Venezuela and Colombia. We were associated in Guatemala, Chile and one of the companies in Venezuela, but the partners chose not to continue with the Group for different reasons. Of course, we also started several operations as sole proprietors, for example, in Argentina, El Salvador, Costa Rica, Panama, the United States and China. The size of our investments is quite varied, depending on the area we can cover: from small bakeries that cost three or four million dollars to those that amount to 60 million dollars.

However, I must acknowledge that the Group has also made mistakes, from which it has learned, capitalizing on the experience to improve its operations and its entry into new markets. Among the most critical missteps were: *a)* errors in appraising different markets, despite supposedly good research conducted in the area (complete lines of products that would sell well didn't work); *b)* entering markets in which sales never reach reasonable levels because the price of our products is high, yet fair. This has been influenced by the instability of local economies since, as we know, several of the countries we have entered have suffered economic decelerations and devaluations, which have affected us mostly due to losses in exchange rates.

We are trying once more to venture into Europe. I say once more because, as I mentioned before, we already had five bakeries in Spain over 60 years ago. In addition to Spain, Portugal, and the United Kingdom, we are now present in many countries in the region through Bimbo QSR.

In Europe, we started to penetrate the market modestly. In 1998, through the acquisition of Park-Lane, a candy distribution company based in Hamburg, Germany, primarily engaged in distributing chocolate in Eastern Europe, mainly Russia, and in Asia, particularly in China. For this company, we purchased two modern production plants in mid-April 1998: one for chocolate in Vienna, Austria, and another for gummie bears and candy in Ostrava, Czech Republic. We ended up selling them because they were not productive enough. In the case of Austria, we appear to be the first to have invested there, and in the case of the Czech Republic, we are second, right after Grupo Alfa. We bought two modern facilities that failed and were taken over by the banks due to the contraction of the economy in the former Soviet Union. Sometime later, we had to divest from the operation in Austria, as it was unprofitable.

This growth, which seemed to be extremely important, was overshadowed by the development that Grupo Bimbo had during the brilliant operation carried out by its CEO, Mr. Daniel Servitje, until April 2024.

THE BIRTH OF A WINNER

Marinela was born in 1956 with the name of Pasteles y Bizcochos, S.A. We started by making round cakes, which were not successful. Sales reps told us people were not buying them because they were too expensive. Mr. Velasco replaced them with smaller ones; they were like a pound cake with cream and jam. Since they had no wrapping, they got dusty in the small town Mom & Pop shops but still sold quite well. Throughout time, Mr. Velasco produced three small cakes in Marinela: one called Gansito, another called Bombonete, and the third one called Nito. There was advertising to introduce them to the market; the salespeople started ordering them as "Ganebos" (Gansito, Nito and Bombonete). Shops would order three trays or twenty trays of "Ganebos." But gradually, they stopped ordering Ganebos and started asking for five trays of Gansito, two of Nito and one of Bombonetes. And so it was that we realized that our top-selling product was Gansito, and we started investing in it. The original wrapper was a sleeve with cardboard on top, with a little metal hoop to hang it. It cost 80 cents, which was very expensive; then we had to raise it to one peso and, when necessary, to $1.10, we said "No." So, to avoid that price increase, we started by removing the cardboard and the hoop and automated production since the product had been made almost entirely by hand; the jam and the cream were added using bags. Nowadays, they are even arranged automatically; there is no more manual work. We were able to make 10 million Gansitos in a week. Without a doubt, Gansito was born as a winner, which we then protected and cared for.

In 2007, the Mexican Postal Service surprised us by issuing a Gansito commemorative postage stamp, which moved us profoundly. It was the first time in Mexico that our postal service had issued a stamp for a commercial product, and we are immensely honored that it was one of ours.

Chapter 2
Factors that fostered our growth

THE VALUE OF EFFORT

One might think that the answer to our desire for happiness is to live a peaceful life without pressure and effort; experience indicates otherwise. If we ask people to share an experience they remember with pride and satisfaction, they generally talk about something that involved overcoming a challenge, a time when they worked relentlessly or made extraordinary efforts.

Based on this, I think that although we seek happiness in recreation and peacefulness, what truly satisfies us and makes us happy, regardless of how much effort or sacrifice it entails, is accomplishing something.

I believe that only those who make an effort and save resources will actually see their work rewarded with financial reserves. These reserves will allow them to face life with greater peace of mind and enjoy the deep satisfaction of having done something right.

Our trust in Mexico

Trust in Mexico was, in fact, the core factor propelling the Group's growth forward. We never thought of going back; we always moved forward, sometimes taking actions that could seem illogical or harmful to the business.

When we started producing bread, we distributed it in Mexico City. Then, we opened routes to Puebla, Morelos, Hidalgo, and Veracruz states. Several of the routes we implemented represented more significant losses than gains. We called them "routes to grow roots" because we did not earn money but gained a market. We thought the market was more important than the money in the long run, and we were not mistaken.

INTEGRATION

To preserve quality and supply, we sometimes have had to integrate vertically. When the consumption of Gansito started growing, we had problems with the strawberry jam. When our demand grew, jam suppliers could no longer provide us with enough products, and they started selling adulterated products, which would sometimes arrive at our facilities in good or bad conditions. As per our total quality policies, we could not allow this situation to continue, so we decided to venture into the production of strawberry jam, and to this end, we installed what nowadays is the largest packing plant in Mexico, in Zamora, Michoacán.

Something similar happened with our flour suppliers until we were offered the Wonder operation in Mexico for sale, which included a mill. After taking over the administration, we discovered that we could operate more efficiently with this mill. This is how we started our new adventure in mills, and in a few years, we became the largest miller group in Mexico.

We also established a metal-mechanical manufacturing operation to produce racks, pan carts, and displays. We require a large number of displays, both for new stores and to replace existing ones that break or get dirty. We manufacture these items with excellent-quality robotic equipment at incredible speed and an unbeatable price. Young Mexican engineers also developed our electrical distribution vehicles.

Our desire to grow. Territorial expansion

Our desire to grow became an obsession, which we satisfied through territorial expansion. We opened bakeries where necessary, always seeking to expand to better serve our customers and consumers.

In a previous chapter, I commented that we never dreamed of such enormous growth. As of the date of this new edition, 2024, Grupo Bimbo is in 35 countries, among others: China, India, Kazakhstan, Russia, Turkey, and South Africa. In Europe, besides Spain, it is in France, Italy, Portugal, Romania, Switzerland, the United Kingdom, and Ukraine. This has been the work of my nephew, Daniel Servitje.

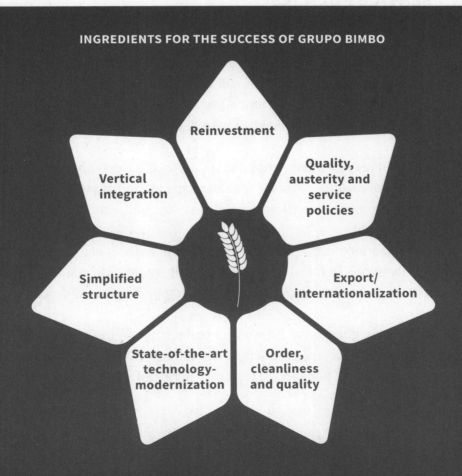

REINVESTMENT

Reinvestment represented a decisive factor in our growth. There is no growth without resources; shareholders' resources are finite because they cannot continue investing forever. Aside from loans, the only source of financing is the reinvestment of profits. The Group has grown consistently; even though the dividends we grant are modest, the value of our shares grows due to reinvestment policies.

MAINTENANCE OF QUALITY, AUSTERITY AND SERVICE POLICIES

Austerity and service are two highly relevant factors for the Group's growth.

Let's start by analyzing austerity. A company that squanders its resources on luxuries and a flashy lifestyle will be unable to maintain a permanent place in the market or a continuous growth rate. At Bimbo, we strive to be austere, invest where we need to invest, and save on what needs to be saved.

Austerity does not mean stopping spending but spending without embellishment. We seek to invest more than to spend, and austerity has helped us keep our expenses low. If we spend less, we will earn more and have more cash to grow.

Although service is not a direct trigger for growth, it acts as an indirect generator. Everyone in the Group knows that if we provide quality products and good customer service, they will feel happy buying and selling our products.

If we provide good service (product replacements, freshness), our consumers will search for our products above all others. Ultimately, all actions directed at improving our service result in increased sales, which is directly related to growth.

Line Diversification

When we achieve the highest share within a market segment or line, we investigate whether we can satisfy the other needs of the same customers. This, in turn, leads us to create new products, such as Takis, which has been a huge success. We always plan to produce the product lines that we commercialize and not distribute other people's products, much less distribute them with our brands if we do not make them.

Delegation

Even with everything mentioned above, even if we wanted to, it would be impossible to do everything ourselves. Therefore, Bimbo has always sought to delegate tasks to associates prepared to carry them out, under the principle of subsidiarity. Knowing how to delegate is essential for growth since more people can do more than a small group working alone could ever do. Managers must delegate their tasks so that they, as leaders, can also grow. The issue of leaders and delegating will be discussed in greater detail later.

EXPORTING/INTERNATIONALIZATION

Incursions into new markets were the determining factor in our rapid and dynamic international growth, which began when we acquired the bakery in Guatemala. Exporting from Mexico and other countries where we have bakeries also helped increase sales and, hence, grow.

ORDER, CLEANLINESS AND QUALITY

When I started to work in Bimbo, my work did not entail great administrative qualities. At first, I was in charge of the sales area. Then I was in the treasury, then the cash registers, and sometime later I undertook the leadership of the vehicles area. As the company grew, the trucks suffered many crashes and breakdowns, and there was no one to handle that. Since I had been an aviation cadet in Canada, and they taught us aviation mechanics in school, I had some experience, plus a great interest in that area. So, I studied the situation and completely reorganized the vehicle department, where I worked for seven years. I was then appointed Sales Manager of Panificación Bimbo and, finally, the General Manager of the Guadalajara operation.

As of that moment, my participation in the Group became more important.

Since I arrived in Guadalajara, I noticed that the cleanliness and order of the bakery were different from what we were used to in Mexico; there was greater attention given to order and quality, which was somewhat criticized because it entailed costs. Now, I can proudly state that I achieved the goal of matching the quality levels of all the bakeries we had back then to those of the Guadalajara bakery. However, the levels between this bakery and the others were considerably different. Currently, all our bakeries and plants are truly impressive in terms of order, cleanliness, and quality; most operate according to the ISO 9000 standard.

Another change that I ascribe to myself is the modernization of the company. It was not an easy task because the older people's mentality was to avoid incurring many expenses; however, we worked to ensure that it gradually became more modern.

MODERNIZATION—STATE-OF-THE-ART TECHNOLOGY

The acquisition of cutting-edge technology and the modernization of bakeries were essential aspects of our growth; nonetheless, growth is based on competitiveness rather than modernization *per se*. When we started exporting, as we mentioned previously, we faced problems due to the different perceptions of quality in Mexico and the United States. Quality standards in foreign countries were much higher than ours, so we had to renovate our bakeries to be able to compete. By doing so, not only did our bakeries improve, but production processes and, consequently, sales skyrocketed. With the increase in sales, costs decreased as well.

Entrepreneurs frequently find their ability to reinvest or invest in technology limited while other organizations grow and improve their processes. In Bimbo, I think we even exaggerated—or perhaps I exaggerated—by doing the opposite. Sure, the benefits are clear now, but it wasn't clear if it was worth the risk back then.

We have an example of these investments in the Marinela Azcapotzalco bakery. We had beautiful cookie ovens in that bakery, but when we undertook our total quality plan, we realized they needed to meet our expectations. Cookies came out golden on one side more than the other, although they were still very good. We looked for the problem with the burners and pyrometers but found nothing. Suddenly, we found that some ovens yielded the quality we strived for. Although an oven such as those we had generally pays for itself after over 30 years (there are bakeries with ovens that are 50 years old), when they were only seven years old, we got rid of them and acquired new Danish ovens, which yielded extraordinary quality.

Another example is our investment in pneumatic systems, which we negotiated with flour millers and conveyor vendors to handle flour that was previously handled in sacks.

Although some measures could be deemed somewhat exaggerated (changes in machinery, annual visits to all the trade shows in the world in search for better equipment, conveyors, mixers and systems), we always endeavored to stay abreast of technology, so much so that our bakeries and plants are at a level that matches or even surpasses the technology of those in the USA, Europe and other regions.

THE STRUCTURE

In January 2008, the Group had four organizations that grouped several companies and 78 bakeries and plants. However, we continued reorganizing the Group's administrative structure to simplify it. In Mexico, we had over 40 regions, which we had reduced to three by 2002. This was achieved through consolidation, that is, a reduction of companies.

We operated with a management system and structure in each bakery.

We had a system of deliveries organized by lines so that eight or nine different Group trucks arrived at commercial establishments to supply various products; this system is quite costly, but it has its advantages. In Spain, our partners pressured us to use another system, which combined cakes and bread in a single route; however, when we tried it, sales suffered.

Currently, due to globalization, international competition, and the economic pressure we are subjected to, we are searching for more affordable distribution methods. For instance, we send a single, sizeable truck to supermarket chains, stocked with the entire product line, instead of seven or eight trucks with different products. Only the driver goes on board that truck and will deliver the products to a GB associate in the establishment. This person will receive and arrange them, sign upon reception, and take care of all the other details related to the operation.

SUMMARY OF GRUPO BIMBO'S SECRETS FOR SUCCESS

1. A crystal-clear idea of what service is. Knowing everything we do regarding price, quality, presentation, products, etc., must benefit the consumer. More than making money, we have always tried to serve our consumers well. I think this has been essential.

2. Reinvestment. Since its foundation, the Company has reinvested most of its profits. When we went public in 1980, potential investors were told that a percentage of the profits was paid out, and the rest was reinvested.

3. Growth. We have always strived to expand. We started expanding abroad when we covered all of Mexico and needed somewhere else. When we covered most of the American continent, we continued thinking of expanding. Therefore, in 2006, we entered China with ambitious growth plans.

4. Marketing. Grupo Bimbo has conducted marketing activities since its foundation, although they were initially rudimentary. What do we mean by marketing? We mean the design of products and their packages, the size of the presentations, the prices of products, advertising, and promotion. I think we were the first bread manufacturing company to advertise; before television, we advertised in cinemas, magazines, newspapers, and through loudspeakers in cars.

5. Fair treatment and permanent respect for people. We seek subsidiarity, that is, the opportunity for the person to grow, make mistakes, participate, and get involved. In short, what we want is for our organization to be highly productive and deeply humane. We are still trying to achieve both. Still, it is a constant, serious concern because we believe that the most important thing about a company is its personnel. The most critical component of its personnel is the leaders. Why? Because they are the ones who select, train, coach, motivate, and inspire others, and they are the ones who genuinely make the Company what it is.

I remember that at the inauguration of a bakery in South America, someone congratulated me, saying: "You do such great things." I replied: "You know, I don't do anything. Instead, I am surprised at what my people do; I sign a piece of paper and look at the amazing bakery they set up." We don't do anything; it is the leaders who are great; they are the ones who maintain the spirit of the Company and take initiative. They can sometimes make mistakes, but they have the opportunity to rectify them.

We are actively developing new products. At first, we offered only four products: sliced, small, large, black (Rye) and toasted loaves of bread. Today, we have over 10,000.

One of the products that makes me prouder is Tortillinas Tía Rosa. Several years ago, when we realized that flour tortillas had good potential and tried to make them, we discovered that there was no automatic machinery to produce them. Thus, we commissioned the engineering department to design one. In Monterrey, a huge machine was built, which was useless at first, but over time, with the advice of experts in the United States, we were able to manufacture flour tortilla lines.

This product ranked fourth in sales for the Group, including sliced bread, large bread, Gansito, whole wheat bread and Tortillinas Tía Rosa.

Factors that fostered our growth 53

OUR CONTRIBUTION TO THE CONSUMER

1 All our products have the highest quality control.

2 Production is mass-produced, in large quantities, automated, and even robotized.

3 Nutrition. In addition to excellent-quality raw materials, our products are enriched with vitamins, iron, and, in some cases, folic acid.

4 Hygiene. All products are sold wrapped and distributed in clean trucks; what is not sold is collected.

5 Freshness. If you, a reader, go to a self-service store and buy a loaf of bread, you know it is fresh. Why? If it weren't, we would have picked it up already. The products have a code, and the sellers know they must comply with that standard without excuse or pretext.

Chapter 3
Our backbone

...so that the company may not only make things with men, but that it may also develop men through things.
ANDRÉS RESTREPO

As I mentioned, those who founded the Group regard it as a community of people working permanently to build a highly productive and humane company. The spirit of our company is built by us all, adhering to our golden rule:

Respect, fairness, trust, and care.

THE IMPORTANCE OF A COMPANY PHILOSOPHY

We can only walk through life with serenity when we understand its supernatural meaning, that is, when we understand and accept that humankind, unlike the rest of Creation, came to the world to transcend.

I am convinced that God made us and placed us in this world so that we can be the instruments through which He can accomplish many things. He could get rid of evil whenever He wanted to; with a single stroke, He could end misery and poverty, but He wants humankind to do that job.

Yes, humans are born with a transcendent purpose: to be helpful and an instrument of redemption for others. If we come to have a good time, live selfishly, do not think of others, and do not love others, we fail to fulfill this purpose.

I participated in a conference at the French University of Montreal. One of the speakers was a Muslim and was sitting next to me. There were Protestants and members of other religions as well. I was surprised by the similarity between Islamic values and our own: we desire the same things. The essence of Islam and Jewish beliefs is similar to that of Christianity. We seek the same goal. Those of us who profess monotheistic religions are not wrong. The teacher, the businessman, and the professional each have a specific responsibility with the elements that God has bestowed upon us and those that we need to develop, we must serve others and fulfill our transcendent mission.

Other religions share many principles of our philosophy. Years ago, I spoke at a conference in Bombay. There were over 500 attendees, and perhaps about 30 of us were Christians. Among us was the scientist who brought about "The Green Revolution," Dr. Norman Borlaug, who is revered in India. We discussed social responsibility and ethical values in the company, which we share with the Hindus and the Sikhs. I believe that the fundamental values of humankind are:

- Respecting and loving people.
- Allowing people to grow.
- Showing solidarity towards others.
- Being generous.
- Thinking that work has merit.

The Christian doctrine has also been able to seize, interpret and spread these values.

The essence of our mission can be expressed with one word: *serving*. To the extent that we have received gifts, we must apply them to serve others, and to the extent that we use them, we will find peace and satisfaction for the duty done. Perhaps worldly happiness is closer to the attempt than to the actual execution; it is closer to the effort than to the achievement; it is the friend of tenacity, perseverance, humility, and love. But, even upon fulfilling our purpose of serving, we cannot expect absolute happiness; life is complex, consisting of happiness and sorrow, joy and pain, successes and failures, all the product of our past actions. Analyzing these actions allows us to learn to live with greater wisdom and grow as people through these lessons.

Just as humans walk through life with a philosophy, so do the institutions we create. Most companies have an explicit, well-defined, and written philosophy. Others still need to have a completely clear philosophy but practice it, yet others practice it without being aware.

However, recent history warns us that in the hard fight for survival, only companies with sound foundations, values, and guiding principles that allow them to gain institutional strength will prevail. A company's backbone is its philosophy, not its organization, systems, or technology, no matter how advanced. That is why, when planning the creation of a company, you must outline your business philosophy.

The Company's philosophy, constituted by the set of values, customs, practices, vision, purpose and the objective of the company, may or may not be in our hands. Some organizations start their operations with a clear vision of what values will govern their behavior, while others weave them along the way.

The Company philosophy, which is composed of ideals and thoughts:

- does not change with the environment;
- does not depend on macroeconomic changes, politics, or commercial blocks;
- depends on the spirit and thoughts of the company's leaders and how they manage to permeate all levels;
- helps the company improve its position in the world. Given the opportunities that may emerge in these times of change, mainly due to the globalization of the economy, economic openness and internal and external socio-political changes, it is essential to have a business philosophy with a rich, deep mystique that encompasses not only the core values but also the main social principles.

It is crucial to develop a clear, illustrated ideology that prominently promotes the principles of solidarity, respect for individuals, fairness, and work values.

Likewise, policies that encourage good manners, foster development, stimulate participation, promote fraternal relations and serve everyone are necessary.

The company philosophy can help attain the first item on the list: promoting good manners and eliciting good habits from all associates. But for that to happen, it is indispensable that the cited philosophy is well founded and encourages the development of people so that their skills, competencies, and culture are allowed to improve. It must also facilitate their participation in different business areas, such as ownership, profits, and fulfillment of functions. Fraternal relationships are promoted when the associate operates in a cordial and respectful environment for the person's dignity, individuality, and opinions. Finally, as it has been created to serve everyone indistinctly, this philosophy will have all the necessary credibility and support. On the contrary, if it seeks the benefit of the few, associates will abandon it sooner or later.

The company philosophy must:

- provoke quantitative and qualitative growth and support reinvestment, investigation, innovation, creativity, dynamics, and long-term vision;
- establish values that may attract people with high ideals and drive away those who merely intend to do business or advance personally. These values will promote integrity and banish corruption.

In the philosophy, we must include the following precepts:

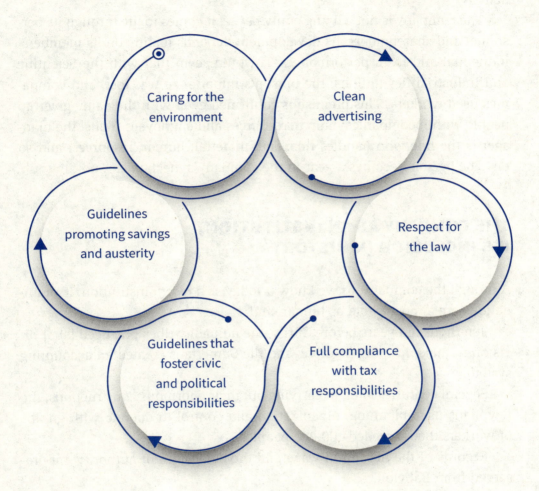

That means having a set of rules that strengthen the company internally and foster the common good.

For the company to fulfill its internal and external responsibilities, its company philosophy must be clear, precise, inspiring, and a guide for all personnel. Those who make decisions must first understand it and live it. Conflict between leaders and associates must be banished, and the community must fight for a fair and humane relationship in their productive activity.

The company is not a living entity *per se*; it comes to life through its personnel and shareholders. Its development depends mainly on its members' individual and team performances. It would seem that with the Scientific and Industrial Revolutions, the person's importance was lost, and companies used workers. This premise is confirmed even with the name given to people within companies: human resources and employees. Thus, the manager is the one who handles financial, material, human resources, and so on. The person becomes a gear in the company's mechanism, not its soul.

THE COMPANY AS AN INSTITUTION, ITS INCLUSION IN HISTORY

Although the company, as we know it today, is a recent institution, its foundations are almost as old as humankind.

Ten thousand years before Christ, the nomadic tribes practiced labor division to make hunting possible, and the Sumerians created an accounting system.

Several centuries later, in carrying out their enormous constructions, the Egyptians used planning, organization and control to operate with groups of workers that exceeded 100,000 people.

Records of the minimum wage and the delegation of authority are preserved from Babylon.

And in our time, banking and double entries in accounting appeared in Italy.

The Renaissance, the Scientific Revolution, the establishment of the first nation-states, explorations and discoveries and Protestant reform gave birth to the Economic Revolution. As Adam Smith explains, this revolution led to the current market system.

At the end of the 18th Century, commercial capitalism, fostered by navigation and colonization, gave way to industrial capitalism, driven by the steam engine. In the middle of the 19th century, financial capitalism appeared, characterized by the preponderance of finance over other areas of existing companies.

ECONOMIC SYSTEMS

The practices mentioned above, customs and techniques led to what we presently call economic systems, which, through their various variations, govern the economic-social functioning of our planet.

Said systems are:

- **Subsistence economy.** The traditional system still operates in marginalized regions.
- **Planned, authoritarian and centralized economy.** The one existing in the socialist-communist world.
- **Market or free market economy.** The one existing in capitalist countries.

Below, we will analyze each one of these systems.

Subsistence economy

More than adhering to an identified economic model, a subsistence economy operates in regions with scarce to null development, and it merely allows for the survival of its inhabitants.

Planned, authoritarian and centralized economy

Socialism, in its various forms, has transformed and conformed to economic and human realities. While many of its principles are good, I agree that others go against fundamental human desires.

Market or free market economy

This system, initially configured as a system known as "economic liberalism," was a consequence of the profound social change brought about by the Industrial Revolution.

TOWARDS A SOCIALLY RESPONSIBLE COMPANY

How to improve the free market system, which seems to be the only one that could work for the good of humankind?

The answer is simple: by humanizing it, giving it a strong sense of social responsibility, and making it good not only for a few but for everyone.

In the case of Bimbo, we have been affiliated with the Unión Social de Empresarios Mexicanos (USEM) since 1963. This organization, in turn, belongs to the International Christian Union of Business Executives (UNIAPAC) and has branches worldwide. The objectives of both associations are the dissemination and the implementation of the principles of Social Doctrine in entrepreneurship. Unfortunately, these ideas are not clear to Western businesspeople. For most, profit is what counts. Most companies have no awareness of these values, not because they are evil, but because of tradition and habit. If we go back to the time of Adam Smith's liberalism, the appearance of the steam engine, and all related changes, we see that companies evolved. First, they were managed by those with some notions of organization, followed by economists and financiers. When guilds were formed, the objectives were clear: to produce at the lowest cost, sell at the highest price and have the cheapest labor (children, women, extended work schedules). Gradually, through unions, socialism, and the doctrine of the Church, a more humane situation was attained. However, the systems called free enterprise do not have a clear social awareness yet; most entrepreneurs from Mexico and the world do not have it.

Once, I gave a lecture at Northwestern University in the United States. They invited me to speak precisely about social responsibility. I arrived on a day that was a holiday for the Jews, and the Dean informed me that he would accompany me to the conference room but that, unfortunately, he would not be able to stay. After introducing me, he sat near the door and never left. He listened to the whole talk. When I finished, the Ethics Director asked me to explain the social issue I had discussed. So, I did, and when I was done, his comment was: "You know? You are right, but this would not work here. Yeah, we need development from within the family, but it cannot be done."

In 1969, I was at Harvard, taking a course that lasted several months. In the beginning, nothing was said about ethics. I discovered that some people had concerns like mine, including a priest who is now a bishop. We got together and asked the Dean: "Listen, the course does not include anything about social responsibility; we only talk about *business*, about how to fight the unions." So, he gave us the opportunity to talk for an hour and a half every week about social responsibility. Attendance was very good, but the truth is that there were things not understood. Most business owners have ethical standards and specific values; however, no clear social conscience exists. And that is the battle, the struggle, the job of the USEM. It is pretty frustrating: after 65 years, very little has been achieved.

Therefore, instead of looking for a third way, which is uncertain and, in my opinion, not feasible, what should be done is to promote a *free market system with social responsibility*.

A market economy with social responsibility guarantees progress, harmony, social peace, and shared development. Those with a universal vision who assess the system invariably conclude that it is good but needs to be humanized.

As Octavio Paz would say: "The market is a mechanism that ignores justice and mercy. We must humanize it."

And, as Ernesto Zedillo, former president of Mexico, would also say: "Mexicans want and will achieve a market economy with a human heart and a human face, with social sensitivity. A market economy that can effectively support those most in need."

In a globalized environment with so many shortcomings and so many opportunities, it is imperative that we supplement our cold market system with one that has a warm approach toward social realities. If we proclaimed that we wanted a market economy but with social responsibility, soon we would question what needs to be done. We would carry out a dramatic transformation, even if it were gradual. This transformation would not only lead to people being less poor but also happier, more responsible, and more productive, leading to a virtuous circle of higher production, greater satisfaction of society's needs and more significant development.

The aspirations and needs of human beings have no limit. When people multiply, their needs increase. On the other hand, natural goods, as they appear at first glance, have only a limited and often perishable capacity to satisfy the needs of humankind.

The so-called economic problem arises from this evidence. How can we increase the usefulness or potential of natural goods to satisfy growing human needs? The answer to this question is through companies.

Companies are fundamental institutions of economic and social life, and they arise precisely to provide a solid solution to the problem above.

These institutions are integrated by the following factors:

- those that provide an entrepreneurial spirit, managerial ability, long-term vision, innovation, and operational work;
- those that contribute capital to achieve both external and internal economic and social goals.

A company's economic and social objectives, both internal and external, are inseparably linked as a joint invention of human beings to serve other human beings. The organization must seek all those goals and harmoniously integrate them. Thus, it will ensure its healthy existence and become highly productive and humane.

People invented the enterprise to multiply the capacity of natural goods to satisfy humanity's needs. Companies and humans experienced a social evolution toward achieving freer and more humane systems during this process.

Companies constituted and directed by human beings have morality. As legal entities, they have rights and duties toward third parties and the State. For the same reasons, they are also responsible toward God.

Companies, constituted by their leaders, owners, and associates, have a soul and exercise responsibility through their actions. Social responsibility fundamentally represents respect for people: not deceiving them, not taking advantage of them, and not using them. The word *employee* can be substituted for *used*, which we should never do. Of course, we must never use people, customers, suppliers, or associates.

The company must serve society. It serves through its influence in the community, environment, and government relationships.

How does the company serve society?

- By providing the necessary goods and services at the right cost and quality.
- By creating an added value that allows fair remuneration for people.
- By being socially responsible in political and environmental aspects.
- By remunerating the people involved and creating wealth that should be applied to pay taxes and everything else.

On the other hand, every company has a purpose, which is why it was created. This purpose fulfills a double objective that cannot be nullified: economic and social.

For a company to fulfill its social purpose, it obviously must achieve all its economic and social goals.

The socioeconomic system in which a company operates, its surroundings, administrative principles, prevailing customs, and traditions undoubtedly significantly influence its appearance. Still, ultimately, the entrepreneur stamps a personal seal on the organization.

The entrepreneur creates, innovates, brings together, reconciles, multiplies, risks, dreams, produces wealth, creates employment, and makes synergy possible. They can do a lot of good, fail to do it, and cause great harm. That is why we state that the entrepreneur has a great responsibility and must always live up to the great mission of serving well.

Despite the considerable technological and social progress attained, companies still have a lot of work to do to live up to their mission.

> **This is the core point: therefore, companies must transform, not to make things with people, but rather, develop people through things.**

The much-needed transformation of companies will only be possible through their leaders, who, with heart, intelligence, and vision, launch themselves into this work, which requires preparation, awareness, understanding, generosity, audacity, strength, and patience.

Chapter 4
Philosophy of the company

A COMPANY WITH HIGH VALUES AND PRINCIPLES

In this chapter, I wish to share with you, esteemed reader, my concepts and thoughts published in Grupo Bimbo's monthly magazine during my time as Chief Executive Officer (1980 to 1997). I supplement them with the knowledge I acquired throughout my entire experience as an entrepreneur. I hope this is all useful to you; my purpose has always been to provide consistency, substance and training value when conveying my ideas.

PERSONALITY

Each one of us has what we call personality. Some display a weak personality and practically go unnoticed. Some, be it an older woman, a young lady, a young worker or a professional, have a strong personality that attracts attention due to their bearing, look, speech, and attitudes. They stand out due to something special that characterizes them. People with strong personalities generally have soundly grounded convictions and clear ideas and know with certainty what they are pursuing in life. Some take advantage of that force to do good and serve humankind, but unfortunately, some use it to cheat and harm others.

Personality can be cultivated. It is a matter of thinking, meditating, and acting consistently.

EXCELLENCE

It is beautiful to find someone or something we can qualify as excellent. When this happens, our spirit fills with faith, our confidence increases, and we must express our acknowledgment. We recognize excellence when what we evaluate stands out from the usual, shines through mediocrity and goes beyond selfish or bureaucratic attitudes. I wish we could frequently say about many:

- *He/she is an excellent person!*
- *That is an excellent job!*
- *What a pleasant demeanor!*
- *It is a fantastic service!*

The dedication and perseverance we invest in our work, our sincere desire to be useful when we do it, and our willingness to do more than expected bring our results closer to excellence. At Grupo Bimbo, we do not want to be ordinary—we seek excellence!

BEING MORE

Every time we ask ourselves fundamental questions such as "Why do I exist?" or "Why am I here?" we feel overcome by doubt and find it difficult to safely penetrate these fields related to philosophy and the supernatural. Since we cannot provide a clear and conclusive answer, we almost always become convinced that our role and mission is to perfect ourselves and *be more*.

Being more is being better; it means growing in all areas, not only without harming others but also contributing to the common good. If we pursue that path, our inner self and conscience will always make us feel good.

Ideals and objectives

Many people get very little out of life because they don't clearly know what they want. Some want so many things that they don't realize what they are really interested in. Others merely do not know why they are here or what they should aspire to. Experience tells us that the only way to succeed is to define what we want clearly. That is, setting precise objectives and clear and concise ideals. The one who knows what he/she wants, who dreams and visualizes himself/herself as already in possession of what he/she longs for, is close to achieving it. If we sincerely try to define our ideals, we will already be halfway towards achieving them.

Inner peace

This is the most genuine objective of humans. Peace may be the true happiness we long for at the deepest, most intimate level of each of us. Nonetheless, it doesn't come free; we must search for it endlessly, intelligently, and quietly. Peace lies close to reflection, simple and constant effort, in the ability to know how to give, in the morality of intention, and far from those who put their selfishness first, who only strive to receive, who do not know how to listen, who will not forgive. Unfortunately, there are many who, in their pursuit of true inner peace, believe they can find it by satisfying fleeting ambitions and whims, which only bring them despair and frustration. Inner peace is a delicate gift that only flourishes within a calm and peaceful conscience.

In the famous novel *Jonathan Livingston Seagull*, I read, "Be careful what you pray for and ask for when you pray because it will be granted." Our Creator put us in this world but will not give us anything; we must get what we want. So, deep down, if we pray and ask, we strengthen our willpower so that what we want will happen. I believe it is granted to us because we work hard for it.

THE PRICE OF SUCCESS

It is safe to say that most people yearn for progress and success. However, only some are willing to pay the price. In my opinion, this price consists of:

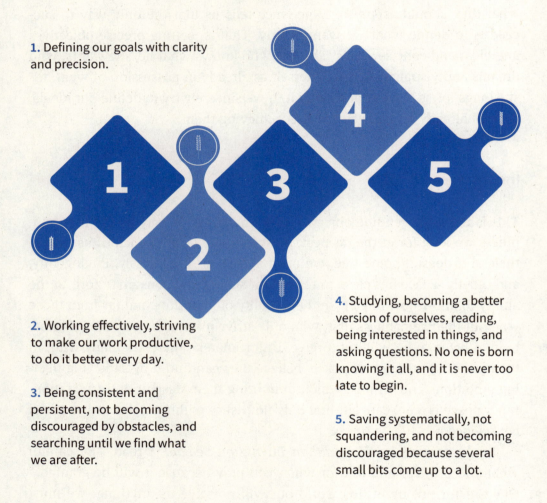

1. Defining our goals with clarity and precision.

2. Working effectively, striving to make our work productive, to do it better every day.

3. Being consistent and persistent, not becoming discouraged by obstacles, and searching until we find what we are after.

4. Studying, becoming a better version of ourselves, reading, being interested in things, and asking questions. No one is born knowing it all, and it is never too late to begin.

5. Saving systematically, not squandering, and not becoming discouraged because several small bits come up to a lot.

Although little is apparently achieved, and the effort seems massive, I guarantee that we will have made a lot of progress and achieved success over the years, almost without realizing it.

SOCIAL ASSEMBLY OF MEXICAN ENTREPRENEURS (USEM)

Our company was forged through hard work continuously searching for the best way to serve well.

In 1963, my brother Lorenzo and I joined the USEM, whose objective is to:

> **Unite, guide, and motivate company leaders towards constructing a fairer, more humane company.**

Through contact with other businesspeople at USEM, we learned about the high principles and values of the Christian Social Doctrine, embodied in several pontifical documents that reaffirmed in us a series of principles that have helped us guide our daily decisions as businessmen and draw the core policies of our business philosophy. USEM instituted the Social Training Course for Business Leaders, which consists of 34 conferences and round tables about the main principles of said Christian Social Doctrine:

- The dignity of the person
- Subsidiarity
- The common good
- The value of work
- Freedom
- Fairness

Since then, Grupo Bimbo has established that every vicepresident must attend said course to strengthen their training and ensure, as much as possible, our company's congruence with these high principles and moral values of a universal nature.

In essence, Christian social thought maintains that we all need the advice of others, human fraternity, and mutual help. Workers must actively participate in the company where they work to become an authentic, humane community where they can participate in the ownership, benefits, and management without losing the necessary unity of direction. The rationale behind this train of thought states that the associate must be a partner and not a silent executor; that person must not be a simple instrument of production whose dignity as a human being is not sufficiently acknowledged, who is not given a chance to exercise his responsibility, express his initiative and perfect himself.

We have supported our philosophy of associate participation in the company, which is based on the principles of the dignity of the person, the value of work and subsidiarity.

One must try to transform the company with a clear idea of what we want, a philosophy, and an ideal of change. Those undertaking this task soon discover that solid foundations are required, supported by universal principles about humankind. Here, Christian Social Doctrine, almost unique among humanistic philosophies, appears as a rich source of inspiration.

CORE PRINCIPLES AND BELIEFS

Different from animals and the rest of creation, from an early age, human beings start assessing a series of moral principles which, with time, become their own and which, together with other convictions, make up their scale of values. If asked what I understand by fundamental values, I would dare answer that they are those a person must be willing to give their life for if necessary. These values guide behavior and willpower, providing dignity and strength to the person and giving meaning to human life. True values not only make a man great, but they also keep a society healthy. In my case, first place in my hierarchy of values are:

- My faith, my religion, my God.
- My responsibility, my relationship, and my dedication to my wife, before my children, before my job. Children go away; mine have already married and left, and my wife is still with me.

- My relationship with my children.
- My job.

Other values of great importance for me are:

- **Probity.**
- **Honesty:** this has many names, but they all mean the same thing.
- **Work** is the only thing that gives a person dignity. If someone doesn't work, whatever they do, even if they give all their money to people experiencing poverty, if they do not generate something for the benefit of others through sheer effort, with their work and intelligence, they are parasites who do not give to others.
- **Respect** is the set of family and personal values, such as respect for others.
- **Integrity** is universal and fundamental. How can someone be trustworthy if they are not faithful to their spouse, cheat at work, or do not help those they are obligated to or need to support?

Integrity

One of the most beautiful virtues of human beings is integrity. Integrity defines a person, group or society that strictly adheres to its highest values.

A person has integrity when consistently practicing fairness, equality, and truthfulness. Those who steal, take advantage of their position, deceive, or take advantage of others may never be trustworthy. Unfortunately, there is more corruption than integrity in the world. What is worse is that governments have led the world in this shameful direction, and many sectors practice corruption, sometimes without even being aware that it is a disease that seriously damages our society and our country. Many problems that plague us nowadays are the direct or indirect result of corruption. It won't be easy to eradicate; doing so is past due.

During my visits to the Group's bakeries and interactions with managers, I repeatedly hear comments like: "What do we do to ensure the Company always preserves its values?" "What do we do to avoid straying from the path we have taken, perhaps with some success?"

Without false modesty, the Group has made progress in this order of moral and social aspects.

Our relationship with labor unions is essential. At Harvard, they taught a class on how to defend ourselves against unions. I was impatient with the teacher: "But what you suggest is to foster a relationship between opposites! It speaks of a class struggle."

Company Philosophy

- We actively encourage respect for all people, expect fairness in all actions, and promote trust and care.
- We strive to maintain a work environment of honesty, integrity, and truth.
- We are mindful of our advertising; we resist the temptation to make commercials with content of violence, sex, disrespect, or vulgarity, although it may be argued that they sell more. Our unwavering objective is that our advertising is not offensive to anyone.
- We comply with all environmental principles and requirements, and in some respects, we go beyond what the law dictates. We are strengthening our relations with our suppliers. We want to be fair and not abuse them due to the high volume we buy from them, as sometimes happens in other companies. We want to maintain a "win-win" relationship.
- We respect the legitimacy of unions. The unions we work with are strong, and they defend and understand their role. We can state that they are honest, transparent groups, and I am sure that only a few companies or even countries do the same.

Our opinion is completely opposite: the relationship must be fraternal, one of collaboration, work, care, help, and support, not of fighting. Unfortunately, human nature requires setting limits, and the union is useful in fulfilling this function.

In our way of thinking, a labor union is necessary; it must be acknowledged, supported, and respected. It must be a clean and honest representation that is professional, capable, and seeking collaboration. Of course, it will stand for the rights of its members, and it will fight and seek the benefit of its people, but it will do so with honesty. In response, we collaborate intensively in its development. We support them openly, with courses, with respect and acceptance. In every bakery and plant, there is an office for union representatives.

Our relationship with the labor union is excellent; it is vital with over 152,000 people working in the Group. If our working relationship were not adequate, we would face countless problems. In many companies, labor is managed poorly through a relationship of opposites rather than collaboration, which yields harmful results for the organization.

Our efforts have been rewarded: in 1994, ANTAD, Asociación Nacional de Tiendas de Autoservicio y Departamentales (National Association of Supermarket and Department Stores) granted us the award for Best Supplier, in 1996, *Expansión* magazine mentioned us as one of the most admired companies, and at around that time, the international company Arthur D. Little informed us that we had been chosen as The Best of the Best company worldwide and that we would have to go to Boston to receive the award. All of this creates a legacy for the Group, which, on the one hand, is quite encouraging but, on the other, compels us to be consistent with the image that people have of us. I must say that we receive acknowledgments that encourage us and make us proud year after year. In 2024, the company was included in the list of the Most Ethical Companies in the World of the Ethisphere Institute for the eighth consecutive year.

The dignity of the person

This is the core principle or value, the origin of all other social principles such as solidarity, subsidiarity, freedom, common good and fairness.

It is also the principle upon which all societal actions must converge.

As mentioned, humanizing socioeconomic systems is a pressing need of our time. Economic development must always seek human development, and human development must always be the driving force of economic development.

Considering the individual as an end rather than a means makes a difference in the lives of humans, companies, and countries.

If we treat others as "things," we "objectify" ourselves. We lose the person-to-person relationship that favors mutual growth, exchanging it for an object-to-object relationship, which is ultimately the origin of most of humankind's evils.

My brother Lorenzo commented once:

"Hey, we are so lucky! As I was talking with an associate of the Group, I realized that besides being intelligent, loyal, and professional, he has high family values and deeply respects his wife and children."

"I think it's not luck," I replied, "it's very important that we attract this type of people and do everything we can to create and maintain a healthy environment."

We intend to live in our corporate family with people driven by values similar to ours—their leadership results from their integrity and ability to direct and obtain results. We are talking about positive results for everyone: the company, consumers, and our personnel—in short, for the common good.

The principle of respect for the dignity of the person means that an individual has the right to be respected while at the same time having an obligation to respect all others. The principle of the dignity of the person reaffirms being human because he/she is an individual, gifted with reasoning and willpower, created in the likeness of God and with an eternal destination. Due to this dignity, people must respect themselves, respect others and demand respect. Being a person gives you the right to shape your destiny and participate in the company where you work.

All team members must understand and experience the dignity of each person. To do so, they must first understand individuality, respect and reciprocity.

- **Individuality** helps us understand that each person is different; however, this does not imply that a person should be treated differently from others.
- **Respect** is an observance or consideration toward people. It can be demonstrated in many ways, one of which is respect for others' individuality. For example, respect for skin color, race, place of origin, gender, height, or any other factor of individuality is related to the understanding of human dignity.
- **Reciprocity** is propitiated by mutual respect and understanding of each other's dignity.

Solidarity: sharing versus competing

Much of humanity's current orientation is toward competitiveness. From childhood, in school, sports and in our homes, we are taught that we must be better than those around us.

Our personal fulfillment would depend on our ability to succeed above all others; that is, we can only attain success at the expense of the failure of others.

However, that is not the case. Happiness is conditioned by a person's desire to improve, not by competing but by sharing with others.

Family, school, and society must reflect on and change that competition model, replacing it with one in line with human dignity. We must strive so that our efforts to succeed bring us together instead of dividing us.

The principle of solidarity demonstrates our character as a brotherhood and our obligation to support and help each other. Solidarity is shown not only when the other person faces great problems, is in disgrace, or cries out for our help. It entails understanding the other person's condition and wanting to help them, even when they do not ask for it. Empathy, service, cooperation, solidarity, and the willingness to share.

Before we can support someone or work with them on equal standing, shoulder-to-shoulder, it is essential to understand what they feel and why they feel it, to understand their motivations and objectives. Once we establish empathy with someone, it is necessary to be willing to help them by serving them, cooperating, and sharing with them. It would be pointless to understand how a person feels if we had no intention of helping them. In short, helping in solidarity may be carried out by:

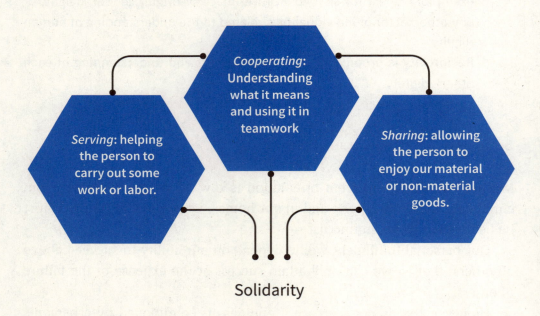

Empathy means "walking in the other person's shoes," understanding what they think but assuming their role from their perspective.

Due to its capacity for social influence, the company can promote this principle of solidarity in its community. For example, in 1995, a challenging year for the Mexican economy, we distributed the document transcribed below among our associates to involve them in the thoughts and actions we considered necessary in that moment of crisis. We preserved the colloquial language to make it clear to everyone.

WORRYING OR TAKING ACTION

We are all worried about our countries' economic landscapes. But since there is no point in worrying, we must comment on what should be done.

Of course, not all of us must do the same thing, as there are some individuals with more direct and specific responsibilities, but there are things that we all must do. It is necessary:

- Work with twice the effort; be more efficient... countries with healthy economies have a profound respect for productive work.
- Be mindful of spending; carefully analyze what we spend our money on. This is a moment for forethought and austerity.
- We must be informed, aware of events and determined to express our opinions. Let us remember that people deserve the governments they have.
- Respect and demand respect for higher values. A society that allows and accepts corruption eventually corrupts itself. A society without values falls prey to low instincts, disorder and attitudes that do not elevate and debase. A debased society cannot progress; it only declines.

Under such difficult circumstances for Mexico, we must not devote time to sterile criticism but to continued positive and creative efforts. In this Organization, despite our hardships, we have faith, are pushing forward, and want to help build a better Mexico.

SUBSIDIARITY

Problems are for the soul what food is for the body. Thus, the worst theft that could be committed against a person is to steal their problems.

Andrés Restrepo

The principle of subsidiarity promotes the possibilities of human development and advocates for allowing the actions of those at a lower level while those at a higher level only intervene when necessary.

This principle governs the relations of all subordinates with their managers or superiors. It implies not only that the person at a higher level ought not to do what the person at a lower level can do well but also that the former should do only what is necessary while helping and stimulating the latter to do as much as possible by themselves. This kind of relationship must operate in a company, between teachers and students, parents and children, rulers and those governed.

HAPPINESS

It is clear that all activity done by human beings is aimed towards a primary goal: finding happiness. It is equally clear that many people never find it. This occurs mainly because they mistake the terms; they believe that happiness is pleasure, cheerfulness, and joy. Others look for it directly without realizing happiness is only obtained as a consequence. It is the satisfaction that is felt when doing and completing those simple and noble things demanded from us in everyday life. We will find happiness if we do what we should do, if we are where we should be, and if we expect what we should expect. First, let us calmly comply with what we feel is our calling, and all the rest will come to us.

THE VALUE OF WORK

It is customary to say that humans live to work or work to live. The truth is that a person is forged through work.

The principle of the value of work, of enormous transcendence for the full development of everyone, establishes that only work makes a man worthy. It states that when earning a living, human beings must do so by planning their responsibility so that the associate is very clear about what is expected of them. His responsibility in the performance of his work must derive from an established plan; thus, the satisfaction of work will not only stem from its results but also from the very fact of doing it, of creating something, of being useful, of putting in motion the abilities and the skills of the person who works. Hence, this person must have much to say about the task performed, which is precisely the importance of their participation.

The value of work has two faces: one for the associate and another for the leader.
On the one hand, the former must feel happy and satisfied with their work; it is important that their work is valuable to them.
On the other hand, the associate's work must be valuable to the leader. If the associate does not show that his work has an added value, it will have no value for the leader.

Similarly, it is unfair for the leader to disqualify an associate who did a good job or applaud if the work was not well done.

To fully appreciate the job, the leaders must clearly understand the work that the associate does within the company and its impact on the company. Leaders must evaluate the work transparently. The associates must have no questions about their role in the company and how their job affects it.

When associates know how their work affects the company, they value it; that is why it is so important that the individual be given recognition and clear instructions on how to improve their performance.

When associates are satisfied with their work, they will do it well. If done well, the person will be more productive or contribute further ideas to improve their work. The advantages are unlimited.

Humans work to live, but as their basic needs are met, they also strive to build a future and increase their possibilities of personal fulfillment and transcendence. The more a person delves into both aspects, the sooner they will see that the only way to achieve them is to be helpful and, therefore, more dedicated to society. They will also see that the most cherished desires of happiness will only be fulfilled to the extent that they can persevere in their efforts to provide service to others.

Although it is difficult to accept that man's economic activity is as healthy and as necessary as others, it is essential to recognize that it is a fundamental function, a moral and social obligation, as well as an indispensable activity for a full and harmonious life, and it is becoming more so every day. Consequently, economic activity—previously scorned and relegated by some as a servile and inferior activity—is today seen as the instrument quintessential to achieving a higher goal: human and social development. Economic activity brings all of humankind's resources into play. Their results depend on their quality, quantity, and intelligent management. Therefore, this activity, which was first unknown, then despised, and a century ago carried out with guilty liberality or absolutism, must now be well understood and better applied because, since the human being is its subject and object, they must be performed as the height of his dignity.

If we disregard an academic definition, we can define economic activity as that which humanity does to create and preserve wealth, using all their resources and applying their intelligence to transform, multiply, create and keep everything they require for their physiological, psychological, or cultural needs, whether they are tangible goods or intangible services.

Nonetheless, humankind's significant innovations, which set milestones in history, were possible thanks to the fact that capital goods were allocated as a result of economic activities. Great buildings, epic feats, navigation, discoveries, and everything we know as progress and development must have been financed with the work and savings of many people. The drivers of change paid for the inheritance of modernity that we now fully experience. The Renaissance, particularly the Italian chapter, was paid for and given to us with resources from the great Roman and Florentine patrons.

GREAT THINKERS AND MANAGEMENT CONCEPTS

Throughout our Company's history, we have encountered great thinkers and concepts of administration through books, conferences, and comments. We have taken some ideas, practices, and recommendations from them. After a thorough team analysis, we have modified some habits and forged our culture.

Some of them mentioned below may help you, dear reader, to have a broader horizon in the continuous changes we as businesspeople must face.

Peter Drucker

For this thinker, the associate must:

- understand what he or she does and feel interested in it;
- understand what happens around them on the job;
- know that they are a member of a work community and enjoy respect and consideration. The associate must also be aware of the possibility of participating in decisions within that community;
- feel integrated into society;
- feel proud of their job and be convinced that their job can make sense;
- not be interested merely in the wages but also in their job, where they work and in the product processes;
- consider the bakery as if they were a manager;
- be deeply motivated to know as much as possible about the business.

Charles McCormick

He was one of the businessmen who contributed to developing the philosophy of participation in Grupo Bimbo with *The Multiple Management Method*.

Rensis Likert

Likert taught us that the hinge organization chart offers more opportunities for associates to participate and become involved than the traditional one. Therefore, we adopted it for our management meetings.

Douglas McGregor

In 1966, we learned of McGregor's work, his concepts on the human side of the company, the limitations of authority, the interdependence in modern labor relationships and his famous X and Y theories related to personnel behavior at work.

Without question, the concept that left the most significant mark on us was Participative Management, a particular delegation method in which subordinates of all levels acquire greater control and freedom of choice regarding their accountability.

Participation refers to a subordinate's greater influence on matters within their superior's responsibility.

McGregor maintained that participation motivates subordinates. They feel satisfied when they discover that they can face and solve problems successfully, obtain the recognition of their colleagues and leaders, and experience that they are independent and in control of their destiny.

Lincoln Electric

In addition to those mentioned above, our philosophy was also influenced by the participation experiences of the Lincoln Electric Company from Cleveland, Ohio, which were described by one of its founders in the book *Incentive Management*. To this date, the participation designs of this company continue to be among the most advanced in the world. Delegation of functions and direct incentives are widespread. Autonomous teams operate with broad responsibility, with plans for profit sharing and substantial access to capital. Lincoln Electric is highly competitive thanks to these programs and its policy of continuous stimulation of productivity. In addition, Lincoln Electric offers its personnel better pay than other industries in the field.

Carlos Llano

Management by objectives, an administrative technique introduced in the seventies, was also one of the elements that contributed most to our philosophy of participation. Carlos Llano of the Instituto Panamericano de Alta Dirección de Empresas (IPADE) [Panamerican Institute for Top Management] taught us that management by objectives, on pain of being a deception, must take participation seriously. His fundamental precept is that more participation must be granted for better decisions to be made, which will yield better results, bringing about greater satisfaction.

In order not to be alienating, work must facilitate man's self-fulfillment, which is not attained only when he achieves his goal but rather while working to achieve it. The widespread dilemma of "living to work" or "working to live" is false because one only lives fully and rationally when one works.

Another of Carlos Llano's concepts is that all work, regardless of how elementary it is, has managerial aspects, and hourlies must be allowed to exercise them as much as possible. This, as you can see, fully supports participation.

Shigeru Kobayashi

Sony's company officer also provided us with some excellent ideas about participation. Kobayashi insisted on making work significant and having trust in people.

Scott Myers

The ideas of this company officer from Texas Instruments company were particularly useful to us. From his book *Every Employee is a Manager*, we picked up the concept that each employee should consider the company as his own and feel that he or she is genuinely working on their own. Below are some of his main points:

1. **People are not against change. They are against being changed.** Knowledge of this premise indicates the importance of helping personnel to change. Often, a company's personnel do not deal with change well because they do not understand what is happening, so sharing information is essential. As associates understand what is happening in the company, change will become easier. They must perfectly understand what is going to change and why. Once they know it, they should learn, in due course, the project details: when, where, how much, etc.

2. **All tasks can be improved.** If associates and leaders understand this, the path to change is facilitated. Deep down, we know that everything can be improved; however, this is challenging to accept, especially if someone else wants to improve our work. Suppose leaders and associates understand that everything can be further perfected. In that case, we will have the opportunity and the right to give our opinion on improving the work of others and to accept recommendations about our own.

3. **Each associate has the essential ability to improve their work (*Kaizen*).** Nobody is better than the associate to do his/her job; therefore, the associate must change and improve it. Frequently, leaders and managers make the mistake of wanting to modify how their associates perform their work without having enough knowledge about what they do.

4. **People like to improve their work and find satisfaction in what they do.** Although it may seem strange, the most effective motivator is indeed personal satisfaction for a job well done. One might think it is the money we receive for doing our jobs, but it is not. The top motivator is satisfaction. Therefore, we must give people the power to optimize their work, be responsible, and give them the authority to improve some aspects or processes of their work.

5. **People like to participate in groups.** As Latin Americans, we are known for preferring individual development over group performance. Nonetheless, we have a strong sense of belonging to a group. We like to be in the family, school friends, and work groups. Hence, motivating people to form participation groups within the company is important.

6. **The most significant improvements at work are achieved by those who carry them out directly.** As the saying states, "Nobody knows better than the ladle what is inside the pot." It is impossible to explain this better. The associate doing the work knows best what is happening, how to improve it, when to make changes, and when to wait.

7. **Help must be given to associates to acquire the basic skills to improve their work through training, coaching or orientation.** Whatever you want to call the process of changing the current condition of an associate, in which they lack some skill, knowledge or experience, they must receive the training, coaching, or orientation that suits them best. This process is mandatory to improve working conditions. The most important thing is to provide the associate or leader with the basic tools to perform his job, and this is not solved by sending all personnel to group training or motivational courses.

8. **The supervisor's role is that of an advisor, consultant, and coordinator.** Born with the wave of the traditional organization chart, where the customer is at the bottom of the entire organizational pyramid, and the vice-president is above everyone, commanding left and right, the supervisor must change his role. The supervisor is the person who oversees. Supervisors have always been to ensure that workers do their work, obey and do not waste time; that is, all their job entails is punishment and pressure. The new role of the supervisor consists of helping, answering, and orchestrating.

As advisors, supervisors must show the path and how to follow it. Likewise, they must address people's questions and know more than their subordinates, but they do so to guide them rather than obtain power.

9. **The role of the associate is to be the manager of his/her area of responsibility.** This concept may be the most difficult to grasp fully. We consider the manager as the individual who oversees a group of people; they coordinate, direct, or manage them. If a manager oversees their group, we can say that is their responsibility. If the manager only has two people to oversee and many other activities to do, the responsibility will be on these two associates, plus all those activities that they will have to direct, communicate, manage, improve, etc. Finally, if the manager had no associates but still had all those activities, we would arrive at the following point: even without associates, one can be a manager of our responsibility.

Tanner and Athos

Tanner and Athos published *The Art of Japanese Management in 1982*. It confirmed our ideas about the value of personnel in a company, the interdependence between everyone who works there, and the convenience of involving associates as much as possible.

Sergio Reyes

Sergio Reyes, the Mexican business consultant from Grupo Dando, significantly contributed to our philosophy of participation. His guidance on democratizing the exercise of authority, considering feedback, and making interpersonal relationships more flexible was highly valuable.

His concept of situational leadership, derived from the theories of R. Tannenbaum and W. B. Schmidt, was a true revelation for us because it enabled us to carry out participation projects that adequately facilitated our staff's professional and human development and maturity.

Situational leadership indicates that the "greener" the associate is in terms of the tasks assigned, the more information and control they will need from his leader. That is, the subsidiary work of the leader will consist of leading the associate by hand. This is usually required when associates are new, when those already in the Company are assigned a new responsibility, or when work systems are modified.

As this maturity increases, control decreases, and the leader even opens the door to functional participation. He can delegate broadly, as associates are already entirely mature. The lack of control does not imply licentiousness but rather total freedom. They will do their jobs on time and correctly.

Tom Peters and Robert H. Waterman

One of the extraordinary books that fueled the traditional management revolution in the latter part of the last century and which inspired us to change our vision to prepare for the future was *In Pursuit of Excellence*, by Tom Peters and Robert H. Waterman, published at the end of 1982, selling five million copies in its 15 translations.

When Bimbo was born, our original plan was to operate a healthy company where associates were respected, with certain levels of quality, but not with a high level of excellence. "Excellence is for General Motors, for the big guys," we thought.

But Tom Peters said: "You can be great too, with your current size or any other." We made a drastic change, undoubtedly a change of mentality. In the past, we used to say that we sang badly but loudly. Then came the inspiration of excellence.

Of course, it costs work and money, as shown by the following example:

We started to make a new cookie with a machine made in Austria that cost a million dollars, a fortune back then. We installed it in Marinela, Mexico, and after a few weeks of working with it, the number of cancellations of that product began to increase.

Our rule is working with losses below one percent. But they went up to four, five, seven percent in that case. We received many complaints regarding quality. We discovered that one day, a salesperson came to see the production supervisor and commented: "Hey, the customers say that the cookies are very pale. Let's see if you can make them more golden," and without further ado, the supervisor went and raised the temperature of the machine. The intense heat made all the iron plates twist, and the machine broke down. They called the head of the Maintenance Department, who, in addition to telling me what happened, added: "The machine is over; if we keep working with it, we're going to have cripples and poor quality." And where was all that excellence? Well, it went to the trash along with the million-dollar machine, and to get back on track, we had to buy another one. In the past, we would have thought: "Tough luck," but this time, we didn't because we wanted the change to be total.

Other works that address the concept of excellence are *Working Smarter*, edited by *Fortune Magazine* and *Passion for Excellence*, by Tom Peters and Nancy Austin.

Philip Crosby

Philip Crosby's fourteen steps for *total quality* led us to carry out a specific plan signed by all top leaders, managers and a large part of the staff in March 1985. This measure constituted a turning point in Grupo Bimbo's history regarding our vision, way of working and management. Crosby's teachings became an essential tool for attaining excellence and solving all the export-related problems we faced.

For this purpose, we created an administrative structure of leaders and training programs. At first, we did not make significant progress, but we continued reading the works of other thinkers, combining various concepts of total quality, and gradually, we continued to progress.

We concluded that, in essence, *total quality* means:

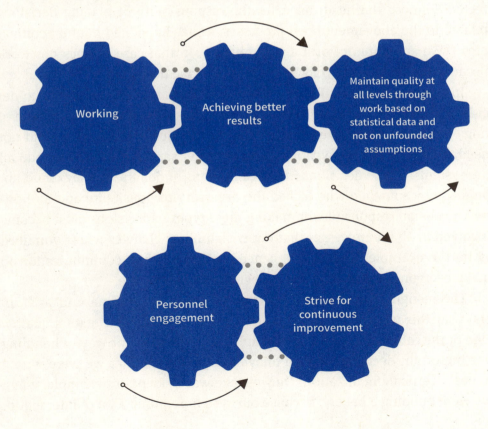

Kaoru Ishikawa, Joseph Juran and Edwards Deming

Further down the road, the thoughts of Ishikawa, Juran and Deming, specifically those captured in the book about the latter written by Mary Walton, guided us in our Quality Plan. The ideas were communicated to all the leaders through seminars and readings. We insisted on training the leaders and on analyzing systems and processes. That led us to reengineering processes since we understood, as Juran points out, that leaders have "85 percent of the responsibility." In general, errors are not due to associates but to systems, processes and how people work, which are designed by management in the end.

In these total quality and reengineering processes, we concluded that the heads, or rather the head, must be convinced and participate more directly. Suppose the head delegates the responsibility of making decisions related to the abovementioned processes, as has happened in other companies ("We are going to form a committee"). In that case, it does not work because the head is the only one who can make decisions.

In the case of Grupo Bimbo, when we requested external advice to decide whether to enter into reengineering, they presented us with several huge proposals. One stated that we had to fire 5,000 associates we did not need, which, of course, we did not do. Another said that we had to redo all the systems. Those decisions involved millions of dollars, so they could not be made by someone who lacked the necessary responsibility and authority. The person responsible for making these types of decisions must become involved in all the processes that imply significant changes where you need to be the example, in which you need to have strong communication to make everyone realize that you are serious, that it is true.

The reengineering process contributed some extraordinary ideas. I always say this was the *bulldozer* that encouraged us to achieve total quality. One of the things that had a remarkable influence was our way of handling our important decisions, which allowed us to realize that we were wrong to use a vertical organization. Our mistake was evident, for example, when we were building a bakery, because our system required a lot of interaction, and this caused important delays in the projects. When we noted that this should be managed horizontally as a process, we appointed someone to oversee its coordination and all the rest. When we did this, we managed to reduce the year and a half it took to build a bakery, from the purchase of the land until the sale of the first product, down to some 10 months. We took the United States' Bell company as an example to do this. Upon carrying out the company's engineering review and realizing that the installation process of a new telephone, which began when the application was received and ended when the phone started to work, took an average of 14 days, Bell undertook the task of reducing that time to one day only. This improvement was not twenty or fifty percent, but rather 1,000 percent.

That made us realize that some things must be thoroughly reviewed. Bureaucracy and tradition make things happen in a way that might not allow us to compete with those who seek to do things.

Indeed, reengineering forced us to make relevant changes. We comprised teams of six or seven people who traveled worldwide for more than a year and then met to review all the processes and systems. This allowed us to become a modern company; otherwise, we would have been left behind.

Jack Welch

In the last decade of the 20th century, the thoughts of Jack Welch, President of General Electric, helped us discover new ways and practices to achieve our company vision.

His book *Control Your Destiny or Someone Else Will* enlightened our vision during the decade, which was practically the beginning of our international expansion.

Chapter 5
Towards a transformation of the company

May work be more than just a task, but a mission, a passion and an adventure. To this end, the associates' goals must be the same as their leaders. Only then will they fully assume their responsibility and give the best of themselves.

Lorenzo Servitje

THE NEED FOR TRANSFORMATION

In order to reach its goals and be guided by the principles analyzed in this book, the company must be transformed worldwide, particularly in Developing or "Third World" countries. It must do so economically to obtain good results and, very significantly, in the social aspect.

How can one transform the economic aspect? Implementing, living, and making the studied concepts come true; for example, reengineering is a powerful tool in the search for total quality and excellence. To achieve this, superb schools guide businesspeople in this direction in many of these countries. Nonetheless, except for the USEM and its equivalents in some of these countries, in the social aspect, there is no institution whose primary objective is to guide businesspeople toward the values that we have analyzed. Much has been written regarding how administration tools can help transform different companies, but more needs to be said about how they can be transformed based on social principles and doctrines.

When seeking social transformation, a company must begin by writing its goals, code of ethics and corporate philosophy. If it doesn't do all this, it will move without direction or focus, in an old-fashioned way, trying to cheat on its taxes, pay its workers less than what is due, or deceive the public because its only objective will be to make money, pay debts, and move the company forward.

Therefore, regardless of the company's size, its top management must decide how it wants to operate socially. They must establish norms, such as "We want to be an honest, fair company, with good participation," and other social elements.

At the same time, they can declare, "We want to be a company that does not pollute. We want the company to participate in politics, make its voice heard through the appropriate organizations and pay its dues and taxes."

To carry out a transformation, it is first essential to outline the objectives.

It is essential that companies, regardless of size and activity, have a clear idea of their objectives in all areas, especially in the social sphere. The clear and precise definition of specific objectives has greatly inspired many to understand their social responsibility.

Companies have a decisive influence on socioeconomic life. They influence people's level and quality of life, the economy, values, development, politics, and social peace. In other words, healthy, efficient, and responsible companies that operate with harmony, quality, and productivity contribute to a healthy and positive society.

Conversely, inefficient and irresponsible companies that do not respect great values and whose members work in conflict are precarious, unproductive, and conflictive, and ultimately, they foster an equally unhealthy and negative society.

A healthy society can't exist if its companies are not healthy. Sooner or later, the consequences of a short-sighted, selfish, and deaf business attitude toward organizations' inevitable responsibility towards all members of the society where they operate start becoming evident.

Actually, the main social principles are the principles of natural law consistent with human psychology; therefore, they cannot be violated if a healthy society is desired.

This is the reason for the resounding failure of pendulum systems, which have exacerbated some of their postulates even though they violate humanity's fundamental rights and aspirations.

Some people think that freedom means everything is allowed and that associates are "free" to work or not under the conditions imposed on them. Still, these people ignore or do not want to see that unemployment, misery, and the most pressing needs force associates to accept working conditions that can sometimes be deemed subhuman.

On the opposite extreme, some think that people cannot properly structure themselves in society. They believe those most favored would misuse freedom to the detriment of the least favored and require a strong, totalitarian government to impose equality, plan all aspects of citizen life and limit personal freedom in favor of the majority.

As we know, these pendulum systems are in the process of becoming extinct.

Both systems exhibit corruption, abuse, and a lack of empathy from society's leaders. Unfortunately, the principles previously referred to are not present in that panorama but are evidently violated. Thus, it should not surprise us that the world cannot live in peace when the selfishness of a few prevails over the interests of the unprotected majority.

All of this shows that every person who lives in society should be clear about the need to behave responsibly towards their fellow citizens and towards all that social life entails because a harmonious social life may only be conceived through the premise that the members of that society must behave responsibly and be aware that they must respect, rely on and—why not?—even show appreciation to their peers. Common sense tells us that every person has rights of different orders and that we must respect them if we want ours to be respected.

It is also clear that human activity can only flow effectively if it is carried out in a warm and reliable environment.

Furthermore, society can only function when there is a code of ethics, laws, regulations, and customs that allow for a healthy combination of the principles of order and freedom and when these rules of coexistence are followed.

Given the previously mentioned scenario, the company must be a breeding ground for the development of all these concepts. The reason is simple: we spend much of the day in the company, to which we usually dedicate more than half of our active lives.

Thus, we can conclude that the businessperson meets several important functions, including:

- being the person who assumes authority in the company; providing a service defined by the set of goals set by an organization;
- having a range of responsibilities encompassing the group the person is a part of and all of society;
- being responsible for the use of the company's assets; therefore, they must see to it that these are used with the maximum efficiency and the highest efficacy possible;
- as a leader of people, coordinate and inspire associates, encourage their participation in the company, and stimulate them to improve personally and professionally;
- making sure that the added value is distributed fairly and equitably, in accordance with the development and continuity of the company and based on the rights of investors, technicians, associates, suppliers, society and government;
- as a person who participates fully in civic and political life. In the same way that one recognizes the need to be responsible as a person, the company, made up of human beings and directed by them, also acknowledges that it must act according to morality.

PROBLEMS ARE OPPORTUNITIES

Many people bless misfortunes or problems because they see them as opportunities to improve themselves and face the realities of life.

They are right; dealing with crises, becoming great in the face of problems, learning from them, and regrouping, given the inevitable forces, allow the person to mature, become strong, and find paths and previously unthought-of solutions. This is because, in fact, big solutions stem from big crises. Creative possibilities emerge from what was apparently impossible.

Times of crisis are bad for pessimistic people who lack the ability to dream. But, at the same time, they are good for optimists who see them as a challenge, an opportunity to mature, and a source of new hope. The need to modify the structures, laws, institutions, and customs that govern the company to adapt to an emerging society better prepared, better informed, with aspirations and desires more defined than those of its predecessors is evident in Latin America; however, it is also a fact that many of the young people in today's society view business activity with distrust.

On the other hand, civilized people demonstrate responsibility and intelligence in their ability to readapt without letting problems progress until they become too difficult to solve. However, in the current era, in which efficiency and productivity are more necessary, our productive mechanisms must show agility in adapting quickly. Our world's famines are mainly due to low personal productivity, not only because too many people are dedicated to tertiary and quaternary activities but also because those dedicated to primary and secondary activities are inefficient.

Contrary to what many assume, the lack of productivity and effectiveness is not due to employees being lazy or incompetent but to the system, leaders, or leadership style.

This is why unlimited opportunities constantly open up for businesspeople who can unleash each person's hidden potential.

Trying to operate in a crisis environment without being willing to adapt is suicidal, and unfortunately, many large and small companies do this. They have yet to understand this new leadership. They debate and fight desperately, no longer striving to consolidate and progress but to not disappear or die slowly.

The failure of some companies in this struggle has a single explanation: *the traditional company is inefficient by nature*. Formal, authoritarian, structured administration always suffers from the vices of bureaucracy. The attitudes of everyone, or almost everyone, are of conformity, less effort, and a lack of commitment. In more severe cases, there is disinterest, resistance, and conflict.

Finding more practical ways to implement and live an entrepreneurial philosophy that aligns with the highest principles is necessary. Given the problem of wanting to do something but not knowing how, many of us have felt that encouraging participation is a safe way to approach the experience. Why participation? Firstly, it is eminently human: no one wants to be outside the team, not play, just a cog in the whole mechanism.

We all want to know why and how we do what we do. We want to contribute not only with our arms or intelligence but also with our emotions, creativity, style, and responsibility.

The system of contracts and wages, job division, little information and little or no participation does not fit human nature; it contradicts and attacks it, which is why it does not work. It is inefficient and does not allow for personal fulfillment; instead, it promotes alienation.

THROUGH PARTICIPATION

We all know that nowadays, Japan dominates international markets with a series of products that, until recently, were almost exclusive to other countries. For example, we have watches, televisions, automobiles, and photographic cameras; it is well-known that Japan controls a high percentage of this market.

This Japanese *miracle*, which allowed the country to compete with the German, Swiss, and American industries as the former market leaders, has its roots in some principles that the Japanese practice relentlessly.

Below is the list and an explanation of those principles.

- **They are focused on perfect quality.** Leaders and associates alike combine their efforts so that their products maintain the specified quality. A defective product is not allowed to go on sale.
- **They work together,** knowing they are responsible for their company's and country's future.
- **They are well-informed** about the company's objectives, goals, and plans.
- **They trust and have a deep loyalty** to their company because they know its future is closely linked to theirs.
- **They have many other positive characteristics,** such as discipline, perseverance, precision, and restraint.

Japanese companies work like big families. Everyone is interested not in personal benefits but in the common good and teamwork. This work style has many virtues, which we must study and adopt if we want to persevere and maintain our leadership and wish to have a more humane and fraternal work style with which we would all feel satisfied.

At Bimbo, we delve into Japanese philosophy through Ishikawa and total quality programs. I traveled to Japan, visited some companies, and talked to businesspeople. Maybe it's simplistic, but I think the business community's success in that country is due, more than anything, to its respect for people. They do not exclude their personnel when they want to achieve something; on the contrary, they involve them.

Japanese, Korean, and other Asian associates feel part of their company. They are respected and informed, allowed to participate, and deeply involved. They do not watch the clock to see if it is time to leave. They think their company is a place they must take care of; it is a part of themselves and will not fail them.

Since its foundational stages, participation has encompassed many aspects of the Social Christian Doctrine, such as respect for the person's dignity, subsidiarity, solidarity, and fairness. For example, let's consider

information and communication that support respect for the individual by providing truthful and timely information.

Subsequently, functional participation and profit sharing support the principles of fairness and solidarity by distributing part of the profits among associates. Finally, the most advanced stages, ownership and institutional participation, integrate the entire philosophy; associates are partners who help run the company.

Participation also responds to the basic principles of human psychology and the laws of productivity, efficiency, and effectiveness. Although participation is only a tool, its moral and socioeconomic repercussions are so crucial that in-depth study and implementation are essential.

Implementing a participation policy in the company cannot be imposed as a productivity or labor relations practice. It must respond to the changes that the company needs to make to build a new business philosophy that is consistent with humankind's desires for a freer, fairer, and more humane society.

It is necessary to highlight the importance of ensuring that the participation of all company associates is consistent with the unstoppable social transformation taking place.

It is evident that humanity is moving slowly but consistently from less humane to more humane conditions, growing in maturity, culture, freedom, and awareness of its dignity.

People, the superior beings of creation, whose importance lies in the fact that they can transcend regimes and borders of all sorts, have walked, with advances and setbacks, towards their objectives of perfection and fulfillment. Humanity has managed to transcend the regimes of slavery and servitude and, more recently, those of a totalitarian nature. However, it still needs to overcome contractual or salary relationships, which turn the person into another instrument of the vast collection of the company's resources, and the only way in which it can achieve this is through participation. All business owners who, like us, are concerned with the existence of social fairness should encourage its implementation.

Chapter 6
How to make progress in participation

Participation is not an objective; it is a tool to realize the desire that associates are not silent executors but immersed in the company's objectives and needs, becoming part of the overall effort through interest, enthusiasm, creativity and ability.

Participation is the way to attain the principle of subsidiarity, which is indispensable for people to grow and not be manipulated or used.

The word *employee* is a synonym of the word used; using people is something negative that the company should never do. Instead, they must be integrated into the company to become a part of it. This is why we call everyone who works in the Group *associates*. In Grupo Bimbo, we have worked on the concept of participation for many years, but in a somewhat confusing way. Andres Restrepo, a Colombian entrepreneur (may he rest in peace), collected all the ideas and placed them on a ladder, which helped us clarify them.

This was how we found that participation has several stages and that these require an order. They cannot be employed randomly; you must start with the first and follow a consecutive sequence.

The process to reach participation must be carried out in a logical, harmonious, and efficient manner, going through the following six stages:

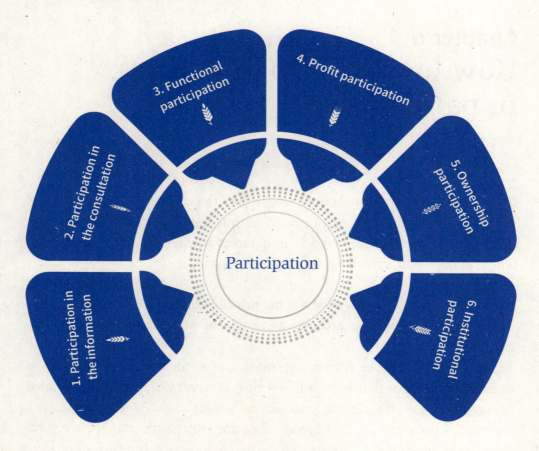

The analysis presented below shows that the first two stages, *information* and *consultation*, are fundamental; the third, *functional participation*, is the core of the process; the next two, *profit* and *ownership participation*, are not as tricky as they seem; and the last one, *institutional participation*, although not relevant or applicable presently in our environment, works very well in some European countries, particularly in Germany.

PARTICIPATION IN INFORMATION

To inform, transparency is required; half-truths are the worst lies.

Participation in information means that all who work in the company, whether small, medium or large, must know everything they need to know to perform at their best. This means they know the plans, the results, the problems, the projects, even the salaries. It is tough to provide all the information, as is the case when providing sex education for children, but it is not necessary to tell them what they do not need to know.

Why is participation in information difficult? First, it is not easy to establish. You need bulletin boards, newsletters and meetings, and an organizational structure that allows communication in several directions: bottom-up, top-down, and laterally. This structure requires order and entails a challenge. Another essential aspect to consider is that total transparency is indispensable for talking. It is necessary to be able to say everything to the right person in the right way and at the right time.

In fact, this first stage is the most difficult because it assumes an authentic decision to move toward a participation plan. That is to say, before taking that step, you must be determined to "take the plunge."

On the other hand, informing, in the sense understood here, implies carrying out four challenging steps.

- Finding the physical means to do it.
- Always telling the whole truth.
- Earning credibility among associates.
- Informing and conveying ordered and systematic information that reaches everyone without distortion.

Although information is distributed with the strictest truthfulness and transparency, almost everyone will initially disbelieve. People with prejudice, not acquired by chance, will require time to become convinced of the sincerity of the proposed participation process and to learn to trust it. However, when this finally happens, it opens a whole new world of cooperation that completely opposes the mistakenly called struggle of the classes or relationships of opposites.

The wonder of this first stage of participation is that it transforms the associates' neutral or negative attitudes, making them receptive and trusting. By achieving this change in attitudes, the associates will also engage and be willing to work towards a common aim. All of this must occur while respecting the necessary conditions.

The means for providing this information will depend mainly on the company's size. If it is a small company, periodic and frequent meetings and a newsletter will work wonders. There must be no gaps in information because if this happens, credibility and trust are lost.

Providing truthful and complete information is an essential requirement. The decision to start a participation plan implies a change, perhaps a very profound one, in previous practices and, as mentioned, it is only advisable to start it if you are determined to act with transparency.

Reporting only what is convenient, deliberately hiding some aspects of a situation, is a way to manipulate people. They can sense or discover that they are being manipulated, which will result in the company losing what it had intended to gain. This could ruin the chance of creating a truly participative company, perhaps forever.

Common sense will indicate what needs to be informed. Communicating the goals, plans, objectives, results, problems, opportunities, and all the information required to avoid rumors and fears is crucial. It is also important to inform them of successes and failures and involve them in strategies so that, consciously or unconsciously, they all work towards a common objective. Furthermore, good communication prepares us for contract reviews, earnings report presentations, and policy changes.

In short, this first stage provides everyone with enough truthful, complete, and relevant information. The company must also be patient and work tenaciously to gain trust.

PARTICIPATION IN CONSULTATION

A consultation is the logical consequence of the good implementation of the first stage. If people are well-informed and trust the information they were given, the next step is to ask them for their opinions on various matters. This way, a communication channel with the fundamentals everyone already knows is opened. The company, for its part, will surely be interested in learning how associates perceive situations and what ideas or solutions they can offer. The result will be that what was initially deemed information will become communication and openness.

Once associates are informed, they have the tools they need to express opinions about topics related to the company. Who knows better how to perform the job if not the associate? Who knows the truck better, if not the driver? Who knows the customers better, if not the salesperson? In this stage, the leaders must consult associates regarding diverse topics. They should ask them for their opinions on the company's actions before deciding. Although they will not make the decisions, the associates' points of view will be considered. Upon reaching this stage, it is important to explain to the associate the mechanism through which the consultation will be made, and opinions, solutions, answers, and questions offered will be taken into consideration; otherwise, they may feel that there is no point in the effort, and they may stop participating. It is necessary to explain clearly and directly how the session will be carried out and its objective. Suppose the leader takes someone's opinion into account. In that case, it is essential to let them know so that the rest are aware and may feel motivated to continue participating constantly and dynamically.

Each stage serves as a foundation for the next. For example, in the third stage, functional participation, the associate must be very sure of their opinions and have all the necessary information regarding their work and the relationships therein. It is essential that they understand not only their job but also how they contribute to the process and one or two previous and subsequent steps.

FUNCTIONAL PARTICIPATION

Functional participation means the associate's involvement and knowledge regarding the aspects of the work area that enable the person to do the job and make certain decisions or take certain initiatives, personally or collectively. The laws of logic indicate that the associate who constantly performs a job knows more about it than many others. If the associate knows the objectives and is capable and motivated, they can correct mistakes and make more convenient decisions when necessary.

Examples of that participation arise daily in a harmonically structured company, and here I will present some specific examples. In 1962, the person making all the decisions in the Group was the CEO. He had his team, usually of five, six or seven top-level people, and he met with each one at different times, once a week. So, we decided to put into practice what we had learned about participation, and we proposed the creation of a "management meeting" where the CEO would continue making the decisions, but instead of meeting in private with each one of his associates, he would meet with all of them every Monday. So, this is how the "management meeting" was established, with an agenda that dealt with the usual issues of daily work, plus additional matters. This meeting fosters teamwork and participation because it allows everyone to know about the problems in each department, preventing gossip, rumors, and doubts. This has a marvelous outcome since decisions are far better reasoned and intelligent. The benefits turned out to be incredible; an immediate advantage is that when a manager is not available, it is not necessary to replace the person right away because any of the other associates is prepared to make decisions for different departments; a long-term advantage is that this prepares those who could become VPs in the future.

Another example of functional participation in the Group is how we address issues related to the large number of trucks in the Organization. In the Group, we have significant courses and a safety training system for the drivers of these vehicles. Although our road accident rate is very low compared to other companies, we have road accidents, like every other company, including crashes, casualties, rollovers, etc. In the past, we dealt with these issues in the traditional way: when there was an accident, the sales manager rushed to the place in question to address the problem with the authorities and others involved; sometimes, in the end, we had to appeal in a trial to determine responsibilities. When the Group adopted the participation method, the drivers, salespeople, and supervisors created a Safety Commission and established their standards. This commission meets periodically to address and analyze the causes of the issues related to the vehicles and propose measures to avoid them. The Road Safety Commission, integrated by associates, is almost always unionized and operates everywhere there are vehicles. In sales centers, with 50 or 100 distribution vehicles each, there is a Safety Commission responsible for addressing road accidents without the support of a supervisor or a manager. There have been cases where the Safety Commission told the driver they could no longer drive.

When associates are trained, informed, and motivated and have the freedom to use their initiative if necessary, very positive results are obtained. The fact that many functions are currently reserved for leaders causes resentment in lower-ranking employees, which can be avoided by ensuring that responsible teams carry these out.

Functional participation is not a panacea but a tool that transforms associates' attitudes and work results. Once the previous two steps have been taken and functional participation is working properly, significant productivity increases will occur, and the company will have people who feel more fulfilled and happier.

A requirement for initiating functional participation is that the principle of subsidiarity be applied, which indicates:

The higher structure should not do what the lower structure can do well.

A healthy application of this principle becomes the main driving force for people's development. It allows them to trust themselves and discover that they can be creative. It makes their initiatives flourish, and their latent capabilities emerge, making them more productive for the benefit of themselves, their company, and their community.

When the principle of subsidiarity is not applied, people are treated like minors, without responsibility, enthusiasm, or trust in themselves, and consequently, the results are mediocre.

Applying the principle of subsidiarity results in:

- the emergence of the interest of each one of the associates;
- increased attention;
- awakened ingenuity;
- enlightened imagination;
- blooming creativity.

If all of the above is achieved, in short, if the associate is treated as a person, the enormous potential in every human being can be released and unleashed. Given these realities, it is difficult to understand why some entrepreneurs and administrators intend to continue operating with obsolete leadership styles in personnel administration.

For example, we have seen associates continue to be classified as "human resources," which implies that people are being treated as resources unconsciously. There is dialogue with union leaders but not with associates; negotiations happen from positions of strength; punishments are imposed; and goals, standards and processes are set from the top, making the associate little more than a silent executor.

A true entrepreneur works shoulder to shoulder with the personnel; the one who dialogues, discusses, and shares with it and knows how to channel their personnel's concerns and desires.

It is worth repeating that the following coexist in the company:

- confrontation and cooperation;
- resistance and understanding;
- struggle and harmony.

And it is in that melting pot that man is forged, authentic wealth is produced, and society develops.

Empowerment

Empowering associates to make decisions (a term that became widely known in the 1990s) reflects the philosophy analyzed above.

Empowerment consists of giving the associate power, that is, assigning responsibility for carrying out tasks and granting authority to do so.

The traditional personnel management model assigns responsibility for certain functions but does not give people the authority to change them. Functional participation solves this problem. It is like empowerment but more elaborate and based on a philosophy rather than an isolated concept.

PROFIT PARTICIPATION

Justice and equity indicate that productivity must be shared, and a healthy way to do so is by distributing it among all members of the production, which includes:

- the *investors* with whom it is shared to improve the performance of invested funds;
- the *customers* or *consumers* with whom it is shared by improving the price of products;
- the *associates* with whom it is shared by improving their income.

However, it is wiser and fairer to share good results when they exist, without this commitment when there are none.

Profit sharing, mandatory by law in some countries, is an excellent instrument for involvement. It rewards everyone when things are going well and sends very clear signals when they are going wrong.

The absolute need to report truthfully, which we mentioned earlier, implies that the company provides this information about the results with absolute transparency. A healthy working relationship and a commitment to associate participation cannot be maintained if associates are not sure the results reported to them are true.

Some entrepreneurs with the wrong vision manipulate the figures they share, mainly for tax purposes, impacting profit sharing.

Others act inappropriately, like the ones above, when they negotiate profit participation by exchanging it for more days in the year-end bonus or some other kind of bonus, even if the actual or altered figures are lower.

Such a suspicious practice destroys the positive nature of this element of participation, undermines its credibility and loses its strong motivating effect. Furthermore, it removes the individual's opportunity to grow and understand that everyone has to benefit from or suffer the consequences when things go well or badly.

It is short-sighted to think that profit sharing is a legal imposition or an annoying problem. Instead, it should be seen as a tool for achieving equity, productivity, and harmony.

Once the right conditions have been established, that is, when a good selection process has been carried out, a good onboarding has been provided, and the necessary training and coaching have been provided to the personnel, great strides will have been made towards having a magnificent workforce, and solid foundations will have been laid for the good progress of the company.

But this is not enough. Excellent communication in the company, fostering dialogue, involvement and participation, and allowing all personnel to innovate, make mistakes and learn from them are also essential. In short, all associates must be allowed to be and feel part of the team.

OWNERSHIP PARTICIPATION

In advanced countries, where the stock exchange works properly, associates can easily access ownership of the company or any other company.

However, discussing ownership participation is difficult in other countries, and little is known about it. Some entrepreneurs from those countries condemn it even without knowing it, others associate it with socialist practices, and most do not consider it an issue that deserves discussion.

I will try to prove that ownership participation is vital for the businesspeople of those countries if they wish to prevail and progress in the new environment around the Western world. But before going into the matter, I will preview some of its characteristics.

- It is not easy to implement.
- It is not something with which we should begin the participation process; it is more of a culmination.
- It is not expensive; it is highly productive.
- It is not a socialist practice but rather the most intelligent defense of free enterprise and the most effective defense against totalitarianism.
- It does not diminish the entrepreneur's authority but legitimates and consolidates their leadership.
- It is not a new adventure; it is growing, generating incredible productivity results.

There are various forms, intensities, and variants of ownership participation. The classic case is cooperative societies, whose fundamental characteristic is that all members own some part of the capital. This modality seems only to proliferate in some countries since the necessary leadership to form a society is rare.

In some countries with a widely developed stock market, many associates obtain shares in their own companies through a stock option plan or directly from the market. This is evident in Colombia and the United States, although most examples of this type of involvement are limited to the highest-level company officers. There is also the case of companies that are born as a society in which all its members are partners to a greater or lesser extent. This case is more frequent and feasible for groups of professionals who come together to form a service company.

One more case is that of companies that offer all associates of all levels the opportunity to acquire shares. This model is, perhaps, the one that should be explored further. As previously mentioned, this type of participation can only occur when there is already excellent communication and other participation practices are already in place; that is when there is a good level of maturity among all associates, leaders and, in particular, supervisors.

There are several ways to encourage associates to save in order to acquire shares or some form of ownership in the company.

One of those ways is called *investment wage*, where associates and the company agree that a part of the wages (usually a part of the salary increases) is systematically deducted and deposited in a fund which, with the corresponding interests, will allow them to purchase shares.

Investment wages are a little-known concept. Essentially, it consists of the additional income paid to associates on top of their ordinary wages. The only problem is that it must be dedicated exclusively to investment, thus remaining immobilized for a certain period. This type of wage has the advantage that it allows for a better income distribution without harming savings and capitalization and is independent of how it is invested. It can be dedicated to long-term loans, bonds, shares, or investment certificates. The fundamental thing is that it does not appear in consumer markets or be hoarded unnecessarily.

One of the pioneers of this form of remuneration for work was Johann H. von Thünen, the German economist of the 19th Century, whose work is unfortunately little known and appreciated. Von Thünen observed that the senseless opposition of classes led the employer to keep low production rates to the detriment of both parties, and this opposition caused the leader to obtain a greater share of scarce products by reducing wages.

His main discovery was that if you take advantage of the enormous strengths of ordinary associates, give them the opportunity and the reasons to increase production and allow them to participate in that increase and in reducing costs, you cannot only achieve a considerable increase in production but also a significant reduction in costs. He also considered, above all, that this increase in production could be achieved at a lower cost if the part awarded to the associate meant savings and ownership for them. It was a noble quest to reconcile capital and labor through a new organization of the company, establishing a salary adapted to human nature. He implemented this plan on his family farm to prove his theory, and the associates preserved the estate thus built for several generations.

Unlike Marx, who took the problem of the distribution of wealth to the political field, Von Thünen kept it in the economic field, and, without a doubt, the history of the last 150 years would have been different if his ideas had been put into practice. His approach, whose main consequence is increased productivity, requires that associates be treated as human beings and that they be integrated into the company. The company itself is viewed as the shared work of investors and associates and not as a place where the fight of opposites occurs.

Ownership participation involves the associate and makes the person feel part of the company. In the Group, we considered this a question of fairness. Still, over time, we realized that the benefits are invaluable and that it is, in essence, a magnificent stimulus for savings.

The only way to create wealth is by saving. You can always save. In my family's case, when we were born, my parents belonged to the low and middle class; however, my mother told us that she always sought savings, no matter how small. You can always do it if you put your mind to it. In the case of associates, profit sharing has been an impressive stimulus for savings.

Many years ago, I found that an engineer always took advantage of the offers to buy shares and had been buying them for 40 years. Because, at that time, they were inexpensive, he had a considerable number of shares. This engineer eventually came to own a significant share of the company. Another time, an hourly whom I had hired 30 years back told me he was going to retire, and he said: "All my children are professionals, I have a small house, and, as you know, I am a shareholder. Hey, by the way, when is one a majority shareholder and when is one a minority shareholder?" He had saved for 30 years, thanks to the opportunity to participate in the Group.

The most important thing is that the people in the Group feel part of the organization. Here, we promote productivity and social peace. People are neither exploited nor feel so, and they believe they are succeeding in life.

In some cases, associates have taken out loans to buy company shares. In others, the Company has compensated them for their seniority so that they can allocate those resources to the purchase of shares. Yet others promote the sale of shares by taking advantage of the distribution of profit sharing, the annual bonus, or any additional income the associate receives.

Although I may sound repetitive, I insist that associates risk their less-than-abundant savings only when the company has achieved trust and participation.

Many companies encourage associates to save and buy shares by giving them some price incentives, subsidizing the amount, or lending them the money at a reduced interest rate so they may acquire stock. However, there is a more important point than that, and the actual benevolence of the plan itself means that paternalistic attitudes are not required. Let us not lose sight of the fact that this arduous process of saving for investment entails a social fund of profound significance. Any economist knows there is only progress with capitalization and capitalization with savings, which are the basis of well-being. The problem is that our people are not distinguished by their ability or their intention to save; therefore, this is where these mechanisms for participation can be applied because they allow and encourage savings, and this, in turn, may help to build a legacy and achieve greater family well-being in the economic, cultural, and social orders, as well as promote family integration over the years. These mechanisms can be considered as an effective formula to escape underdevelopment. If someone out there says this is true but not easy, the person is right. It is not easy and cannot be improvised, but it can and should be a goal if we want a company with a future.

What I have said so far does not mean that I believe implementing an ownership participation plan is urgent or essential; what I am saying is that leadership that allows the involvement of all personnel is urgent and necessary, and for this process to be authentic, it must culminate in the possibility of a full partnership.

Some business owners have questions about the percentage they must offer when considering a plan of this type. This should not be a reason for concern. Unfortunately, we always talk about very small percentages due to the difficulty mentioned above in saving.

Many entrepreneurs would like to obtain a better response from their associates and thus have an additional source of financing.

They have doubts about practical, administrative, psychological, union-related issues, etc. However, there are always paths and solutions when both sides have the will. In many countries, there are countless practical cases of participation.

Some countries also face legal problems because special treatment for "worker shareholders" is not yet contemplated. However, we trust that existing innovations in this subject may constitute transcendental decisions in the socio-economic lives of these countries, which will undoubtedly contribute to increasing productivity and social peace.

Below are several companies in which the participation of their staff stands out:

- In less than eight years, Domino's Pizza had become the second-largest pizza company in the United States. Its service levels are unprecedented, and it is made up of the most incredible group of young people who are involved and excited about their company.
- Mervyn's, a champion company of the Dayton Hudson organization, managed to sell in one week, which took its competitors 13 weeks to sell. When employees from other chains who later joined this one were interviewed, they invariably responded that the change was like "dying and going to heaven."
- Giant Food (Washington, DC) has by far the highest return per share among publicly traded convenience stores.
- Publix (Florida), a retail company, pioneered employee ownership.

- Milliken Co., a textile company with sales of $ $3 billion, introduced an aggressive quality improvement program in 1980, supported by a broad personnel participation plan.
- General Motors' Saturn plant has the most ambitious participation plan in operation to date. It is known as the only resource that can compete advantageously against small Japanese cars. Commentators call this project "*the boldest experiment ever in self-management.*" Saturn workers are total associates.
- Lincoln Electric (Cleveland, Ohio), a company dedicated to producing welding equipment and materials, is almost becoming a monopoly because no one can compete with its prices and quality. Its associates, all partners, receive an annual bonus that adds up to several times the salary they are paid.
- Other examples of these industries are Hewlett-Packard, IBM, Apple Computer, 3M, Campbell Soup, Trammell Crow, Worthington Industries, Marks & Spencer, and Perdue Farms.

INSTITUTIONAL PARTICIPATION

In institutional participation, the unions, which officially represent associates, are part of the company's Board of Directors. Below, we will describe this briefly. This does not imply that we recommend putting it into practice; in fact, it is currently only being used in very few countries with a high level of industrial development.

At the beginning of this chapter, we mentioned that today, this aspect of participation has no relevance or application in our environment; the truth is that we don't know of anyone who has adopted it here. Furthermore, our knowledge of our surroundings and social psychology tells us that it is not something that could have a practical interest for us. However, it is necessary to expand on this aspect, not only out of academic curiosity but also because it is something that we can glimpse on the horizon and that we view as a logical and natural practice when sufficient progress has been made in the processes of human development, maturity, and healthy democracy. From this perspective, it is an ideal to which it seems fair to aspire, albeit with limitations.

Years ago, important entrepreneurs, through the Unión Social de Empresarios Mexicanos de Monterrey, expressed their desire to thoroughly understand the concept of how the participation of employee representation operates in the senior management of some companies in Germany, including Volkswagen. With this idea in mind, they commissioned a prominent professional to study that operation and bring back first-hand information. Upon his return, he was expected to report that this legal provision did not work for large companies and that, although there were joint obligations between the management of the companies and the associates, the actual management occurred in private leadership meetings.

Many were surprised when the results were quite different. Upon his return, he reported that associates' participation in these companies' direction, planning and operation is genuine and highly positive. Decisions are much closer to real life, more creative and, of course, more expeditious. Worker representation understands that there can be no separation between the interests of shareholders, officials, and workers and that the better the company operates, the better the latter's results.

Given that we still need to gain the maturity required to apply this concept in our environment, we could not think of implementing it.

However, this should not prevent us from aspiring to and working towards constructing a freer, fairer, and more humane society.

Chapter 7
A mission and an ideal

At Grupo Bimbo, our mission is the guide for everything we do. Working every day to achieve it and to meet our goals is the raison d'être of our company.

TO SERVE, OUR REASON FOR BEING

At the end of the 1970s, Andrés Restrepo[†], a great friend and renowned Colombian businessman knowledgeable about social responsibility, taught a seminar called *Company Forums* to some of the Company's vice presidents and managers.

In this seminar, we were invited to dream about the company we wanted to build with a human vision. He asked us to create a company tailored to humankind.

The desire to be *a highly productive and deeply humane company arose* almost from the moment we began. Over the years, we have sought a practical way to institutionalize this desire. Andrés Restrepo's seminar inspired and reinforced many of our concerns.

It is essential for companies to have a profound reason for their work!

OUR MISSION

A company must have something that motivates it, injects life into it, and gives it meaning and a worthwhile purpose.

In a sense, that purpose is an illusion that is pursued, a reason.

In Bimbo, that wish was summarized from the beginning in the words **Believe-Create**, and it is expressed in a more straightforward yet more concrete manner in the following note, which we published in newspapers on December 2, 1945:

> **Today, upon starting our operations, we want to communicate to the people of Mexico that we have made it a rule ALWAYS to produce our products WITH EXCELLENT QUALITY. In addition, we will provide our distributors and customers with the timely and efficient service that Mexico City, already a great metropolis, rightfully demands.**

That purpose was the reason for being around which the Company was built. When we established it, we wanted to ensure that the personnel became identified with their work and the Company.

Companies quite frequently seek this identification instrumentally. From the beginning, we thought this mission would give the people who make up our organization an important reason to work.

In my talks to leaders, I emphasize the profound meaning of service: "Who does not live to serve, does not serve to live."

A mission must carry in its core the desire to serve. Only then will it be able to provide enthusiasm, through which the sacrifices that every job requires are better understood: getting up early, visiting customers despite ruthless weather conditions, covering night shifts, working Sundays, and many others.

A mission is actually a company's merging element. We could also say that an organization's soul is its people. Nonetheless, we would not be referring to the number of individuals it includes, but instead to the will and passion each one has to serve. This, carried out as a whole, constitutes the soul, the spirit that drives the company.

In Bimbo's first 10 years, there was no clear, written definition of the Group's mission. Managers were concerned about respect for people, human relations, trust, and care. The concepts were present but not identified in writing. In 1962, when the corporate offices were established, we started drafting all the rules and procedures.

We first drafted the Company's philosophy, summarized in one sentence: *"To be a highly productive and deeply humane company."* When new top management took office some years ago, this fundamental rule was changed to a more comprehensive set of considerations.

The enhanced mission is now expressed like this:

> **Delicious and nutritious baked goods and snacks in the hands of all.**

- Our purpose: "Nourishing a better world."
- Philosophy: "Building a sustainable, highly productive and deeply humane company."

Without a doubt, a fundamental recommendation is that the mission must be stated in writing and that there is a code of ethics, a company philosophy, and an intention of how you want it to work. The mission is the first stone of the building that is going to be built. What the company wants must be written down, even in it is very simple terms.

The two fundamental aspects that must be covered are economic (profits, quality, efficiency, growth, service) and human, which encompasses social relations, remuneration, and, in general, social responsibility (political and environmental matters).

A business mission must be written down because it must be shared throughout the company; otherwise, it will not work. Managers who play some leadership role at any level must know, feel, want, and live with these values. If the leaders do not understand or accept, or if they "pay lip service" to the mission, things will not go well. At Bimbo, when we see that a manager is not committed to our philosophy, we ask them to find something else to do: "You are not going to succeed here," we tell them. The leader, notwithstanding level, must be a person who adopts our philosophy, feels part of it, conforms to the way of thinking that predominates in the Company, and embraces its values. That is the secret of our success.

Although our mission statement has changed over the years, its essence will endure.

OUR IDEAL

Our sense of the ideal is closely related to the mission.

One of the more significant contributions the company can make to its associates is to develop an environment where they can discover and achieve their ideals.

A person without ideals, without dreams, is vitally ill. It could be said that the person *lacks a soul*, something that encourages and moves them.

The company's ideal is expressed in its mission. Likewise, every person must have an ideal, and the company is a very favorable field for them to carry it out. On the one hand, it is through the company that people are paid for the work done, thus satisfying their needs and desires. On the other hand, the company is where each associate can grow by solving problems and relating to others.

Everyone shapes the measures and the ideals that are pursued at Bimbo. Undoubtedly, well-informed and involved people participate, think, and contribute. Here is an example. About 20 years ago, for reasons of productivity and hygiene, we decided to automate the packaging of some small products. Back then, we produced 10 million Gansitos a week. The packaging process required a lot of people, so we thought: "This has to be mechanized." We traveled to Switzerland, Italy, Germany, and the United States but never found the equipment that we needed. One fine day, a mechanic from Guadalajara took on the project, and we managed to automate the machines. It is incredible to see how the products become aligned and arranged and how everything is done without human hands participating in the process.

If our personnel had lacked interest and motivation and were only looking at the clock to prepare to leave, we would never have had the spirit to achieve what we have. There are many other examples like this one, like drivers who know that they must take care of their vehicles, check that the brakes do not wear out and that they should not waste gasoline.

Our people are the Company, and it is due to their strength that our companies have advanced further than our competitors. I believe that without a clear and truly living philosophy, it would have been tough to compete because having it in writing is one thing, but actually living it is another.

> The company is a learning field where the culture and those who shape it influence each other reciprocally.

SHAPING A CULTURE

My questions regarding what we mainly attribute the Group's growth to and what our culture's main features have led me to search for real answers.

I found that the practices that have shaped the culture of Grupo Bimbo and have contributed to the success of our organization are the ten that I will explain below. I will describe them briefly and then analyze the relationship between them and our philosophy. Each practice described is a program our Group has implemented at different times.

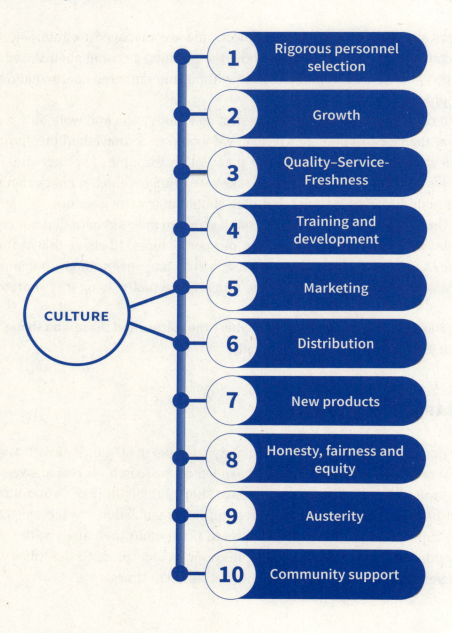

1. **Rigorous personnel selection.** Since the foundation of our company, we have practiced rigorous personnel selection. We search more for attitude than for knowledge.

By carefully choosing our associates, we save a lot of money, guarantee the quality of our products and good customer service, and maintain productivity.

It seems exaggerated to overemphasize what this simple practice accomplishes; however, as I mentioned, we are convinced that the Company will be, after all, whatever its people are, and its people will be whatever their leaders are.

The selection of leaders is, therefore, of particular importance. We ensure they have the necessary intelligence, integrity, leadership skills and ability to relate to others; they are good at collaborating and understand that their responsibility involves having a clear business sense. A leader must not only know how to do his job well, but he must also obtain results.

2. **Growth.** Growing has been a concept of the first order in the Group. Since the beginning, there has been an interest in expanding distribution, releasing new products and lines, and entering the integration business, which we have considered convenient due to quality, uniformity, or other demands.

An important characteristic is that we have never stopped growing, neither in crisis nor when facing aggressive competition. Our rule is to reinvest most of the profits and pay the correct dividends, but we aim to provide the Company with all that it needs to modernize, grow, and take advantage of opportunities.

This policy, which I firmly believe, has been the driving force for development, job creation and our Organization's healthy and robust growth.

We never look in the rearview mirror and have our foot on the pedal to the metal.

3. **Quality-Service-Freshness.** Maintaining these three product principles is our primary commitment to the consumers. We strive to have every one of our products delivered with the best quality and offered with the best service and freshness. The three factors of this practice must always be present to give our consumers the product they want. A good quality product would be useless if, when it reaches the consumer, it is not fresh or offered with poor service.

The advantages of this practice are undeniable. For many years, our products have been on the tables of homes in Mexico and other countries, and they have always been fresh. To fulfill this task, we selectively analyze production, regularly visit our customers, and collect the products before their expiration.

4. **Training and development.** We prioritize personnel development. One of the most common practices is coaching, training and promoting their constant growth. Development never ends; when an associate learns everything about the functions related to their position, we try to help them learn more about other parallel or higher areas.

We constantly apply the principle of subsidiarity.

We want our associates to grow in all aspects. To achieve this, managers must also undergo continuous updating to learn how to implement the principles and philosophy of participation. A good associate becomes better as they learn and develop.

5. **Marketing.** This function has always been a priority for the Group. Since its foundation, Grupo Bimbo has considered it necessary to design products and presentations that consumers accept, paying special attention to their sizes, packaging, and prices.

Honest advertising and interesting promotions are excellent vehicles to publicize and stimulate the sale of each product. The Organization has been meticulous when it comes to its advertising and promotion:

- We ensure that what we state is true and benefits the consumer.
- We insert our commercials and advertisements in television programs that are clean to avoid contributing with our sponsorship to programs with content of violence, sex, vulgarity, or anything else that violates family values.
- We are looking for a clean and family-oriented image. We promote family

activities in which our principles are shown; for example, we support sports and cultural events.
- We never allow our brand to support advertising actions or television programs that are against our principles and values.
- We make sure never to invest in any media that promotes social disintegration.

6. **Distribution.** Grupo Bimbo has aimed to reach all corners where we have established distribution routes. Although some places are distant from what has already been mapped, mainly at the beginning of our operations in a new region, we seek to cover them all. It does not matter if we lose money initially; we know they will become profitable customers in time.

7. **New products.** The Company continually investigates and develops new products so that the consumer always has a more extensive variety to choose from.

We have innovation centers where we review and test all new products before they are launched to the market. We do significant research in this phase because new products are the company's lifeblood, keeping it alive. Before a product launches for our consumers, we conduct market tests to understand their preferences and ensure that the product will be accepted.

8. **Honesty, fairness, and equity.** With this practice, Bimbo reflects in a direct way the most significant part of its philosophy's richness. Our organization invests all our efforts in ascertaining that all associates, leaders, and managers are honest.

We are convinced of the cancer that corruption represents; therefore, we do not grant gifts in exchange for preferable spots in supermarkets, bribe traffic police officers, or pay to expedite permit procedures in government agencies.

We try to be fair and equitable in all our interactions with the union, the government, suppliers, shareholders, our associates, and all others.

9. **Austerity.** Bimbo is a profitable company that does not squander its earnings. A policy of austerity has always governed us. Austerity does not mean avoiding spending money; it means spending what is necessary without luxuries or ostentations.

We do not save money when purchasing machinery, transportation equipment or computer systems. We invest large sums in everything related to improving our quality and productivity. Nevertheless, our bakeries, plants, and offices are areas with everything necessary to work well but without luxury.

This austerity goes hand in hand with savings, and we want our associates to consider it that way. We think, and we have proven over time, that luxuries are unnecessary to meet our objectives since every peso spent or invested must achieve profitability.

10. **Support to the community.** From its foundation, the company has destined a percentage of its profit to social work, above all related to education and the needs of Mexican agriculture. As we are a strong consumer of agricultural products, since our main supplies are wheat, corn, oilseeds, sugar, milk, eggs, cocoa, strawberry, pineapple, walnut, butter and others to a lesser extent, we want to contribute as much as possible to the development and the professionalization of those who dedicate their lives to this primary activity of such great transcendence, which at the same time suffers from so many deficiencies and underdevelopment.

Fundación Mexicana para el Desarrollo Rural (the Mexican Foundation for Rural Development) provide our primary support in this area.

Support for educational projects does not need to be justified. We are convinced that the best investment for any country is made in educating children and young people.

OUR BELIEFS

Throughout history, we have dealt with this matter in different ways. The main objects of our desires and concerns are the customers and the consumers, the product and the people who make up the company.

As we mentioned in previous pages, developing a culture requires more than trying to live with some values or customs; it also requires consciously mentioning them. This is why the language used to present the Company's fundamental principles varies over time. Only then can they remain alive for new generations.

- What has brought us success?
- What do we require for the future?
- What must we avoid?
- Where do we need to persevere?

Given that the Company is made up of its people, the values we aim to reaffirm must be known and desired by all company members, especially the leaders.

In 2010, the Group's CEO considered it appropriate to renew our presentation of our values. The six values were represented graphically with six circles; each illuminated with one of the three primary colors or one of the three secondary colors. These circles, in turn, formed another circle in the center of which appeared, in white, the value Person, the principle that we consider to be the beginning and end of what we do.

When we began to draft this diagram, those of us who were senior leaders of the Group were asked to express some ideas about each of the values instead of defining each. Below are the ideas that we expressed at that time. The first ones are from my brother Lorenzo Servitje, and I consider them motivating and inspiring:

Passion: "We see our work as a mission, a passion, an adventure; sharing this in an atmosphere of participation and trust constitutes the soul of the company."

Person: "Always see the other as a person, never as an instrument."

These are from Daniel Servitje.

Profitability: "It is the visible result of all our ideas, efforts and illusions. It is the oxygen that allows our company to continue living."
Teamwork: "Agile, active, enthusiastic, with our sneakers on, sharing. Learning from everyone."
Trust: "The foundation on which everything is built. Relying on each other for the common task."

These are from Roberto Servitje:

Effectiveness: "Making things happen; results. Serving well is our reason for being."
Quality: "Our company must be creative, effective, efficient, productive and with a very high ideal of quality and service."

In 2015, we started to express them as beliefs so we could embrace them and bring them to life in practice. We believe this makes them more powerful and turns them into actions and behavior models we can follow daily.

Each of our beliefs is mirrored in the activities that define us and make us a humane company.

- We value the person
- We are one community
- We compete and win with superior quality
- We act with integrity
- We get results
- We are sharp operators
- We transcend and endure

We Value the Person

The safety of our associates comes first. We follow the Golden Rule, treating each other with respect, fairness, trust and care. Everyone has potential, so we foster their personal and professional growth. Diversity enriches us, and inclusion makes us stronger.

We are One Community

We are one global company everywhere. We are passionate about what we do, and it shows. We collaborate to break down silos. We make work fun and celebrate our achievements.

We Compete and Win

We are a hungry and driven team, never satisfied and with a sense of urgency. The consumer is our boss; the customer is our partner. We build and nurture brands that connect with consumers.

We Act with Integrity

We think, say and do the right thing. We always act in Grupo Bimbo's best interest. We value each other's good faith, and our behavior builds trust.

We Get Results

We act like owners, focusing on today and tomorrow. We empower; we are and hold each other accountable. We are agile, uncovering and capturing opportunities. We have a "can do" attitude.

We are Sharp Operators

We master our trade, executing with precision and excellence. We do not accept waste and unnecessary spending. We get better and learn every day. We value simplicity and adopt new technologies.

We Transcend and Endure

Profitability is the oxygen of our business. We drive the marketplace, anticipating and embracing change. We are a force of good in the lives of our associates, society and the planet.

OUR VISION

- To make our business a business by being productive and attaining established levels of profitability.
- To increase our brands' volume and market share. Be close to our consumers and customers, who are the reason for our existence.
- To get our personnel to develop and perform fully (to live our philosophy); to be permanently oriented towards learning.
- To ensure our operation takes place in an adequate environment of order (information, systems, and trust), participation and self-control.

OUR CODE OF ETHICS. BACKGROUND

Since the founding of our company, we have sought to govern our conduct by criteria of integrity and respect towards individuals and to be very firm to avoid the temptation of adopting "practical" traditions that encourage corruption and gradually erode company values and trust.

As critical situations arose, we established specific rules and criteria for action. Now that we operate in several countries, we have prepared a code of ethics that governs all our operations. Before presenting examples of our Code, I will comment on some cases we've encountered along the way in which we had to act clearly and firmly.

Some examples are the following:

- Bribes at customs.
- Road traffic violations.
- Relations with labor unions.
- Removing surplus personnel.
- My retirement as Chief Executive Officer.
- Hiring and permanence of vice-presidents.

In the Group, we are profoundly satisfied not only with not giving in but also with verifying, in each case, that we made the right choice since it favored us significantly, as you will see in the cases we will discuss next.

Bribes at customs

On several occasions in previous years, we faced serious problems at customs when importing equipment, materials, or machinery. We were told we needed to "grease some palms" to speed up the formalities.

However, despite the pressures, the long delays and the severe disruptions that this represented, we kept going.

We consistently adhered to the Company policy of not offering bribes or getting involved in situations that could be classified as corruption. Bit by bit, we have now fully solved this annoying situation.

Road traffic violations

The same thing happened when we started selling outside of Mexico City. On the roads, they stopped our trucks, making up alleged violations to try to obtain some illegal gifts. For some time, our drivers would return with tickets for those "violations," which we fought, negotiated, or even paid. Still, we never authorized our drivers to provide the requested gifts. Over time, the members of the police force learned that Bimbo was not participating in any bribes, and they stopped bothering us. There is no doubt that good behavior pays. If we were to calculate the millions of trips we have made without covering those dirty quotas, it would be evident that, aside from fulfilling our principles, we have saved a lot of money.

Relations with labor unions

When we started working, we discovered it was a general practice to "strike a deal" with the general secretaries when dealing with unions. In our company, on the other hand, we established a relationship based on teamwork, ensuring transparency and significant participation of all personnel in contractual decision-making. This has resulted in active, honest unions that seek the benefit of all together with the Company. This fact makes us proud.

Removing surplus personnel

On two critical occasions, partly caused by the "six-year political crises," we faced excess personnel situations. The first time, we had about 1,000 surplus salespeople, and the second, 5,000 associates. The natural response would have been to carry out the essential personnel cutbacks. However, given the pain that such a measure would cause our colleagues and their families and in response to our objective of making a deeply humane company, we looked for solutions that allowed us not to make the massive readjustments.

In the first case, we used the situation to create a new distribution we had studied. We changed the truck signage and salespeople's uniforms and began using them to develop the distribution of the Tía Rosa products. Thus, we converted this apparent problem into an opportunity.

In the second case, because of in-depth reengineering research that revealed a high surplus of people, we had to implement a series of measures that ultimately caused an economic cost for the Company but avoided a severe social impact. During a meeting, the Board of Directors asked when we would fire the surplus personnel. My response was that we would not do it, and I presented a plan that, among other measures, proposed:

- *Checking if there were any questionable personnel*, that is, people who should have never worked in the Company and should be fired. There were very few, maybe 40.
- *Forbidding, in the strictest sense of the word, hiring new personnel.* Any urgent need had to be authorized by the Chief Executive Officer. The vacancies that came up would be covered by surplus personnel, reorienting them, training them, and maintaining the same salary level if the vacancy had a lower salary.
- *Taking advantage of surplus qualified personnel*, directly or through an intermediary, to expand our participation in the international arena. We have always maintained that the limitation in business is the personnel. Ideas, technology, and financing exist or may be obtained, but trained and experienced personnel are limited. In the situation described, we decided to venture more broadly into the international arena.

A surplus of 5,000 people is cause for serious concern. I reasoned that with a 15 to 16 percent turnover with 44,000 associates, most of the problems would be solved in one year; although this would represent an additional cost for the Group, it would be manageable. I always appreciated the Board's support for that decision.

Now, many years after that incident, the Group has grown in sales. We have more than 152,000 associates and better productivity standards per person. It would have been a serious setback to have lost trained and experienced staff, and the morale and confidence of everyone else would have been weakened.

My retirement as CEO

Another temptation I consider we handled appropriately was my retirement as CEO. I had established 1997 as the year in which I would leave the Company's leadership, mainly for two reasons: one was that I wanted to have more time for my family and my personal projects, and the other, equally important, was that I wanted to give younger people the opportunity to introduce the changes required in a rapidly changing and globalized world into the Company.

I sensed that we, the founders, who apparently knew everything, would have difficulty making these changes and achieving the much-needed modernization.

The temptation was that I was asked to postpone that decision for a year or two, but, thinking of the good of the company, I did not accept.

I was happy with my responsibility as Chairman of the Board of Directors. My suggestions and opinions can help the new generation, and I am joyful that my decision was correct.

Hiring and permanence of vice presidents

However, we must also recognize that there were three occasions when we succumbed to temptation when, due to the urgency of filling an important position, we hired personnel who did not meet all the requirements, and we had to pay the consequences. Even though the people whom we recruited on those occasions fulfilled by far almost all the requirements we established (intelligence, integrity, capacity for work, leadership, and a sense of business), they displayed weakness in one area: their ability to relate well to others, to show affection. It took us a while to recognize our mistake, but in the end, these three people had to leave, leaving behind a trail of problems and resentments that are difficult to correct.

OUR CODE OF ETHICS

The principles mentioned in the section entitled "Our beliefs" in this chapter are the foundations of our Code of Ethics, which all company members, especially leaders, must know and live.

It expresses the commitments we, as a Company, must fulfill to the various audiences we interact with.

Below, I have included some extracts from our Code:

Towards customers and consumers

Our customers and consumers are the reason for our existence. Their satisfaction is essential to our success.

Therefore, our primary commitment is to the quality and safety of our products and services.

We uphold the commitment to inform our consumers about the nutritional value of each of our products.

Customers are our strategic partners, so we must strive to make our business proposition one that fosters their growth and development.

Towards shareholders and partners

Our commitment is to create long-term value by providing our shareholders and partners with a sustainable and reasonable return on their investments.

All our business practices and transactions use resources prudently and profitably and comply with the highest ethical and legal standards.

Towards associates

At Grupo Bimbo, we strive to treat all associates with respect in a positive environment that fosters their personal and professional development.

- Each person has a unique value, and we acknowledge that their contribution is essential to their team's performance.
- We are committed to providing a safe working environment and maintaining a safety, health and wellness culture.
- It is our fundamental commitment that where labor organizations exist, their independence will be respected if they represent the legitimate interests of our associates, seeking to establish a relationship of collaboration and mutual benefit.
- There is zero tolerance for acts of corruption.

Towards suppliers

We expect our suppliers to benefit from each transaction so that they can expect sustainable development, improving the value of our mutual relationship in all aspects.

We seek to partner with our suppliers so that we may offer excellent products. Hence, we work with suppliers who guarantee the highest food quality and safety standards.

Towards society

"At Grupo Bimbo, we recognize that our *raison d'être* is the society in which we are immersed; it is to it that we are indebted and for whom we work, which is why we are gladly committed to and support with our work and daily attitudes the principles and values that sustain our society as a whole and, in particular, the community in which we live."

"We are committed to ensuring that our promotional and advertising campaigns promote the strengthening of universal ethical values, meaning family unity, the physical and emotional integrity of people, respect for the universal rights of children, respect for people with disabilities, the elderly or people of any ethnic group or social condition."

Towards our competitors

"Grupo Bimbo and all its associates are committed to competing vigorously and objectively in the marketplace, based on the merits, advantages and excellence of our brands and services, and fair business practices."

In our day-to-day operation

We are convinced that Grupo Bimbo's daily business and operations must be simple and productive. We are committed to following the austerity principle in all our business processes.

Assets protection

"The protection and safekeeping of Grupo Bimbo's assets is the responsibility of each of us who comprise the Company."

Compliance with legislation

"Grupo Bimbo, in all activities carried out by its representatives and associates, regardless of their nature and scope, will fully preserve the spirit and form of the laws in force in the countries where it does business."

We remain informed about the laws in effect in each country where we operate and will make any necessary adaptations to comply with them.

Commitment of the leaders

The Code of Ethics concludes with a commitment before the signature of each manager:

"Grupo Bimbo associates shall respect and participate in those local customs that encourage behaviors by the Group's principles and values. We will not participate in—and we will seek to discourage—those business and cultural practices contrary to them. The Grupo Bimbo Code of Ethics will prevail over local customs and business practices when in conflict."

Since we are present in countries with different cultures and laws, we seek to understand and respect local customs and practices as long as they do not violate applicable laws, contradict our principles and beliefs, or go against what is set forth in the Code of Ethics.

Chapter 8
A company will be what its personnel are, and its personnel will be what their leaders are

IN BIMBO, WE OFFER JOBS, NOT GIGS

When the company opened, we started with ten very neat salespeople dressed in uniforms, including caps and bowties. They drove impeccable trucks. At that time, none of our competitors had uniformed personnel; we were the first. To this day, they continue to wear uniforms and drive always clean trucks inside and out.

What distinguishes Bimbo from other companies is that when a person comes to work with us, they have a job, not a gig. The reader might ask, "What is the difference?" Well, yes, they are two different things. On the street, in the offices, it is possible to see where productive work is being done and where people are just "keeping their seats warm."

We endeavor to prevent anyone from doing anything that is not productive, useful, profitable, or satisfactory. This is because those who only cover appearances cannot be happy; they likely feel frustrated inside. The difference between productivity and satisfaction is significant between doing productive work and simply filling a position. In a favorable, motivating climate, real work benefits the company and the person.

A couple of cases have been written at Harvard University about Grupo Bimbo. When these cases are solved in the executive program of this university, it is common for someone from the Company to be present to clarify questions and make comments related to the solution of the problem.

I remember that once, at the end of our presentation and discussion during the plenary session, a student stood up and asked: "How come these little Mexicans think they can enter the US market, which is the most competitive in the world?" I was about to respond when the university Dean asked for the chance to do so.

After providing valid business reasons why we were able to penetrate the American market, he commented the following: "You [referring to the students] think that businesses are a matter of money. These men [talking about us] have flour in their veins; they love their job and have known it for 50 years; they love their people, they prepare, they know about bread, tortillas, flour, sweets, snacks..."

In the end, time answered the question posed by that young man.

In games and in reality

In 1969, I had the opportunity to study in a program for entrepreneurs at Harvard University. One of the last subjects, Business Management, involved playing a business game. The game was about managing a made-up company, and the decisions made were real. Teams were formed for the game.

One of these decisions, which framed the course of our made-up company and left an indelible memory in me, was when we were presented with a situation in which a problem arose, and sales decreased. Our American peers immediately suggested firing several *guys*. The Japanese classmate and I refused to take that measure, saying: "First of all, they are not *guys*; they are people, and we are not going to fire them." After some discussions with our team, we convinced them not to fire the associates. Later, the market recovered, and we won the game above all the other teams.

They lost because they fired people. When the market recovered, they had to hire and train people again, which took time and gave us an advantage. I know it was a game, but that is what has happened to us in reality.

DEVELOPING OUR PERSONNEL'S TRUST

I remember once when one of our production masters commented to a group of workers: "When one enters this company, we do it with fear that we will be cheated by not being paid what was promised or that we will be set up. We arrive here *tiny*; then we grow and realize things are not so. After a while, we see that we are respected, trained, and treated with fairness, trust, and care."

Beijing

When we reopened the bakery acquired in Beijing, a year after taking it over, one of the associates who had worked there since the Company was founded said in public, among other things, something that got us all excited: "I have been in this company for 10 years, and we had always been promised many things that were never fulfilled. In the year we have been at Bimbo, they have fulfilled their promises, and we are very happy and grateful for this." The importance of the associate can be approached from different perspectives.

For a company leader, relationships with their personnel are fundamental; they represent, without a doubt, one of the aspects of greatest social significance. So much so that if these relationships were managed well, the serious and alarming global problem of antagonism between systems and nations would resolve itself.

Company managers or leaders play a decisive role, not only in the Company but also over personnel because, whether on purpose or inadvertently, they are the ones who model the prevailing attitudes and mode of operation of the Company. In the long run, they are also the ones who make up a unique company. Consequently, when talking about personnel, it is essential to speak of the leaders, and the philosophy that the Company follows since the Company will be what its leaders are, and the leaders will be the result of embodying a business philosophy.

If we accept the principle that leaders shape personnel, we could say this principle is neither good nor bad and that the environment determines their behavior. This is a mistake. Personnel, that is, the people of Mexico and perhaps all over the world, are intrinsically good and respond positively or negatively to environmental stimuli.

However, although the external environment, that is, the prevailing environment in the society in which companies and individuals operate, influences the attitudes of the latter, if two companies are compared, one with a mystique and the other without, it will be seen that they are very different entities even though they have personnel from the same social environment. The following table lists the qualities and defects seen in each.

Company with mystique	Company without mystique
Productivity	Inefficiency
Quality	Mediocrity
Order and cleanliness	Disorder and filth
Efficiency	Losses and waste
Innovation and creativity	Routine and obsolescence
Cooperation	Passive resistance
Fraternal atmosphere	Confrontation
Human development	Alienation
Progress	Frustration
Trust and affection	Distrust and suspicion
Collaboration and progress	Union violence
Human solidarity	Struggle of the classes

A company without mystique is characterized by unmotivated, uninvolved, and even offended personnel and problematic work relationships.

How are these workers expected to worry about seemingly unimportant matters? A place that can give an idea of the atmosphere that prevails in a company is the restroom. If the environment is terrible, the restroom is defaced and graffitied by associates, as this is the way they get even with their leaders. This does not happen, for example, in Japanese companies, whose successes in quality, creativity and technology are supported by the philosophy of involvement. The Japanese associates truly consider themselves part of their company; they are proud of it, and if the company is hurt, they feel hurt, too.

The same happens in other Asian countries. For instance, in Korea, I spoke with a man who worked at Korean Airlines. When I asked about their vacation periods, he answered, *"No vacation. The company misses me. Hard work."* They had no vacations, and their salaries had been reduced. I told myself, "I want to be the director of Korean Airlines!" Yes, people give their lives to the company; that is the spirit one wants to stimulate.

Some Japanese people have very different visions. For example, in an article I read in a magazine, a Japanese man who works in a personnel recruitment company declared: "Forget about other things, the associate only works for the money, that is the motivation. All the rest is nonsense." I think he is wrong; money is significant for the associate, but it is not the fundamental reason. Work does not only give people money, and they not only work for it, and whoever thinks this way limits the person, isolating them in many aspects.

I have observed, with the Group's associates, that people work for many other reasons besides money.

GUIDELINES

If we accept the above, what guidelines should we follow to ensure that the company's personnel desire to act like the personnel in companies with mystique?

The first would be, without a doubt, that the company has a healthy philosophy and a code of business ethics covering, among others, the aspects which are described in the following table:

1. **Producing goods and services which satisfy the needs of society.** We all like and feel proud of belonging to a Group that knows how to build prestige.

2. **Displaying absolute respect for all people.** Respect for a person's dignity has multiple aspects, from the most basic to some that are more subtle but equally relevant actions. A respected person respects others in turn and feels backed up by a solid platform from which he or she can undertake a dynamic development.

3. **Justice must be applied without exception, making it an unalterable norm of life.** There are three types of justice: commutative, distributive, and social. They must also be lived systematically and naturally. Justice is the main ruler of human community life.

4. **Promoting and fostering personal development.** Everyone desires to prosper, but having more does not necessarily mean having more. What really counts is being more… being better.

The company, its environment and its attitudes must promote individuals: they must trust them, allow them to make mistakes and learn from them, encourage them to use their initiative, not fear participation, and make the best possible use of their limited or full capabilities.

A business philosophy that promotes development by acting subsidiarily, intervening only when necessary, and stimulating personal growth becomes a forger of people. Those discovering or validating their potential are more productive, happier, and reliable. Some businesspeople seem blind or clumsy. They complain about the deficiencies of their workforce without considering that what would be amazing is if the associates were efficient in an environment that neglects, denigrates and alienates them.

Many aspects must be changed to make a company efficient. One aspect of this transformation, from less to more humane, is the opportunity to participate at a deeper level.

Participating is a synonym of *being part of*.

5. **Recognizing and revaluing work.** Without using worn-out rhetoric, work is the main dignifying factor of humanity. It is impossible to imagine a society that does not recognize its members' efforts and contributions.

Work is the only thing that sustains man. Without work, human life would not exist. Work is not, as has been clumsily stated, punishment. It not only dignifies but also promotes, strengthens, teaches, and purifies. Only the sick and the very old do not work. Unfortunately, however, parasites who are pretty full of themselves prosper at the expense of others without contributing anything to the society that supports them.

It is essential to recognize the value and dignity of work, regardless of its significance. Work's value is not measured only by its contribution but by its effect on those who perform it.

6. **Promoting an environment of solidarity, emphasizing the internal realm as an extension of the human relations that bind us as children of the same Creator.** It is essential to have a clear awareness of the need for a supportive relationship instead of an individualistic or collectivist one. A company that takes care of the interests of all its members, both under favorable and difficult circumstances, is a company that inspires trust and one to which its associates dedicate themselves without reluctance.

7. **Ensuring that the common good is promoted in all actions implemented.** Just as a society, and I am quoting Joseph Höffner here, "must not abandon its members, but rather take care of them, society's members must be willing to subordinate their interests to the common good. It is necessary that the common good, which until recently was limited to the State, be increasingly universalized, granting rights and obligations encompassing all humanity (*Gaudium et spes*)."

A company with a clear vision of its social responsibilities and mission of service abandons the narrow niche identified with selfishness and meanness to soar above the dimensions of a company that contributes to constructing a freer, fairer, and more humane society. Every person desire to belong to a human group that lives up to these high values in their daily lives, whether conscious or unconscious.

OTHERS STIMULATING TRAITS

I will analyze other characteristics below that stimulate workers' pride, loyalty, and affection toward the company.

Applying and experiencing the guidelines I propose for a business philosophy mentioned in previous chapters must work as a solid launching platform for constructing or transforming a deeply humane company.

However, other attitudes are also necessary, which, for various reasons, make all this conditioning operate satisfactorily and be projected synergistically, integrating an exemplary, harmonious, dynamic, and leader-in-its-field company.

These attitudes are described in the following list.

1. **A dynamic of growth, innovation, and progress must be in place.** It is necessary to inspire a mystic for work, effort, and a fighting spirit. A wealthy or bureaucratic company cannot be constituted. Nobody is interested in stagnation or obsolescence. It is not true that people want an easy job that does not involve challenge and effort; it has been proven that the more demanding a task is for those carrying it out, the greater their motivation and involvement will be.

2. **Having a plan that involves increasing improvement.** Attaining gradual but constant increases in quality and productivity. These are the vital ingredients for uninterrupted development and progress. An expert author on productivity mentioned that it is infinite; I would add that its search is a perennial activity. Even briefly, it must be said that productivity results from implementing a total quality plan in which the necessary tools are used, especially statistical analysis and process assurance. It is amazing to see how the personnel are devoted and passionate when they realize that they can do more and do it better and, consequently, can grow in the economic and psychological fields.

3. **Having a training program.** A program supported by properly refined systems allows each individual to know, be able to and want to do well no matter what must be done. After inefficiency, problems, breakdowns, injuries, variable quality, and so many other evils of the company, incompetence and ignorance from associates about what is expected of them lurk in a corner. Obviously, these associates are not to blame for this situation. If we train them halfway, they will perform halfway.

Serious and complete training prevents errors and unnecessary costs, helps standardize quality, and awakens professional pride, trust and appreciation for the company.

Many of the so-called Third World issues stem from disregarding formal training.

4. **Assuming an attitude of austerity.** Sooner or later, companies experience crises of various kinds. A careful, prudent, and austere organization has a greater chance of achieving tranquility and managing efficiency. Luxury, spending and unreasonable investments may compromise profitability and even the company's endurance. Associates clearly perceive the signs issued by top management in this sense.

5. **Having good profitability.** Being a highly productive company, having resources to:

- pay all involved parties fairly;
- pay taxes;
- conduct research and development;
- carry out development, growth, and remodeling;
- being able to handle emergencies.

This implies having, among other things, the following:

- sound accounting policies;
- inventory assessment systems according to the economy.;
- revaluation of assets;
- depreciation policies;
- price policies;
- retirement and reserve funds;
- reasonable financing and leverage.

A company that is not economically consolidated or lives in constant anxiety in this regard can weaken the morale of its associates.

THE LEADERS' POLICIES

The Leaders' Policy consists mainly of carefully constructing the required profiles in all aspects: labor, technical, professional and personal. Their thinking and personal philosophy must be compatible with the company's philosophy. If, during the initial interviews, we realize that the candidate's values are incompatible with the organization's, we let them know. Prospects are offered a seminar called *Be a Better You Course*. It lasts three days; it is very intense, well-thought-out psychologically speaking, and it deals with personal things, not work. It talks about everything, particularly about the family. If, upon completion of the course, the person says: "It's amazing, but I don't think so; I don't feel the same," we direct them elsewhere. The selection of leaders is rigorous, both in the professional aspects and personal values. I am not speaking of religion or sectarianism but of value awareness.

An example of our values is the way we manage our advertising. As mentioned, we are very specific in that it must be clean, broadcast in media advertising where there is no possible offense to the public, and there is nothing that goes against family values, where there is no violence or sexual content. If a person in marketing does not care about this, conflict will arise one day. Those who work in marketing must decide not only to comply with the rules but to do so out of conviction: "No, I cannot sponsor this program."

LEADERSHIP

> A leader dreams, takes risks and innovates. He or she pursues situations and modifies them when they are insufficient for his or her purposes. If they do not exist, they create them. A leader guides, communicates, convinces, motivates, and helps others identify and desire new goals.

Leadership, a topic widely discussed and studied since ancient times, has a special meaning in our company. Without leaders, we could not achieve our goals. The core aspects of our definition of a leader are principles and philosophy.

To analyze this topic, it is worth asking what happens when there are no leaders at the global level. The lack of authentic leadership is an obvious sign that problems have exceeded the leaders' ability to solve them. Humankind inevitably needs leaders to help it achieve its various goals, frequently help identify them, and instill the desire to achieve them. It is sad to admit that most human beings go through life without knowing precisely what they want.

In his visionary work *The Rebellion of the Masses,* Ortega y Gasset states, "Society is always a dynamic unit of two factors, minorities and the masses." The difference between the two lies in that minorities are characterized "by having some clear desire or ideal" and that "select" minorities are not formed by the petulant individual who believes to be superior but rather by the one who demands more of themselves than others.

Accepting that there are select minorities, those we could classify as current or potential leaders and more or less compliant majorities, the problem we face worldwide is a shortage of leaders who can guide the rest of society's healthy development.

When problems overcome us, there is no doubt that a lack of leadership brings this about, and currently, world problems are overwhelming us. These problems include the following:

- ecological issues of great transcendence;
- energy-related issues;
- inflationary problems that cancel out the desire for progress of the majority;
- lack of understanding between nations and ethnic groups;
- violence;
- loss of values and corruption;
- demographic explosion;
- unemployment and underemployment;
- excessive inequality in income distribution;
- shantytowns;
- extreme poverty.

This last problem affects us and pertains to us as businesspeople. In general, in developing countries and mainly in the Third World, where our balance in productivity is poor, we are inefficient, and a culture of inefficiency has taken root. Some intend to blame it on ancestral issues, but the truth is that leaders, those of us who make decisions, have not managed to organize work effectively.

There is, therefore, a leadership vacuum, a certain conformism, and a desire to be, as De Tocqueville said: "A meek and conditioned society which expects the government to solve all its problems. We know that the wealth of a country is not measured by its natural riches but by the productivity of its people."

As previously mentioned, humankind is made up of two fundamental groups: the minority, which thinks and acts, and the vast majority of people who allow themselves to be led by others, i.e., the masses. The word *mass*, used in this context, is unpleasant to me because it degrades the individual. But humanity is indeed divided into two: those who know what they want and are tenaciously dedicated to getting it and those who go through life as if they were blindfolded. The interesting fact is that those who know what they want are actually a minority.

True productivity does not arise spontaneously; it results from an educated, hard-working society organized by leaders with vision, ambition, creativity, integrity, and solid social awareness. This is why this topic is so transcendent and timely.

If we want to undertake paths that will allow us to advance from the Third World towards the levels of developed countries, we need to have suitable leaders, many leaders, large and small, in all areas:

- in government;
- in teaching;
- in politics;
- in trade unions;
- in intermediate organizations;
- in churches;
- in corporate environments, of course.

We urgently need strong, morally sound, entrepreneurial leaders with a strong social conscience in all environments.

NATURE OF LEADERSHIP

I have always believed that leadership is a gift latent in all of us from the day we are born and that it often develops due to a particular environment or situation.

Now, I am sure that it is indeed possible to develop leadership talent. To a certain extent, it is a quality acquired by those with a clear idea of their desires, tenacity and perseverance, and a keen desire to fulfill them. However, some experts in this subject, such as John Kotter, a professor at the University of Harvard, claim that leadership is a combination of skills, all learnable. Kotter insists that today, more than ever, the world needs leadership.

He mentions that most companies have excessive administration, a lack of leadership, and a great need for change. People who can bring about this change are needed, and there is a surplus of those who only manage.

John Kotter says: "Doing what was done yesterday, and improving it by five percent, is no longer a formula for success."

I had the chance to listen to John Kotter at Harvard, which genuinely changed my thinking. I always thought leadership was something that one was born with, that the person inherently had. But one day, Kotter said, "No, you are not born with it; leadership is something that can be acquired, and that often arises for historical reasons or due to circumstantial pressures."

He gave the example of Harry Truman, who was thrown into the presidency of the United States during World War II and issued the order to drop the atomic bomb on Japan. The man was no leader, but when the time came, he emerged as such.

Peter Drucker, a well-respected and admired consultant, stated that most leaders he has known were not born leaders, and they were not made into leaders, but rather, quite frequently, they became leaders obligated by circumstances.

This would be the case with Harry Truman or with Lech Walesa. In any case, it is evident that we urgently need to have more and better leaders in all environments of our planet.

When discussing leadership, it is essential to address the hierarchy, equality and inequality, as well as the difference between being bosses and being leaders.

American zoologist Robert Ardrey maintains that: "In every animal society, there is a system of domination, a given order of status in which individuals are organized by rank. Everyone knows who is to be feared and to whom they have to give in, but an animal leader, in exchange for its privileges, is the first to face their enemies, run risks, struggle, and, if necessary, die in a fight."

Human society has this same structure. Understandably, any society whose members are not equal requires and favors this hierarchy to function.

Claude Levi-Strauss, the French anthropologist, states that in any human group, there are men who are different from the others, who feel a strong call to responsibility, and whose primary remuneration is the burden of social responsibilities. Thus, a society where members are not equal is mentioned, while we constantly hear talk of an egalitarian society. Behind many social tensions and conflicts, there is a tendency to pursue equality, and the reality reveals inequality.

Part of this serious problem is due, on the one hand, to the fact that all men are equal, in essence, because we have the same dignity, origin and destiny. Still, at the same time, we are existentially different due to multiple and varied accidental factors.

The pretense of an egalitarian society is unnatural and impractical. The only thing that those who have tried to implement it have achieved is a society with more significant differences. The reason is that those who try to impose it in a totalitarian way are even more different, more powerful, and more privileged. They display almost cartoon-like differences, which would be difficult to compare with truly democratic societies.

It is necessary to clearly understand these concepts of equality and inequality so that, on the one hand, they do not obstruct the exercise of legitimate leadership and, on the other, to acknowledge that there is a duty of quality and responsibility to reduce the gap between these differences by evaluating the limitations and shortcomings of the majorities. Those who have received the most in any of the orders undoubtedly have the most significant responsibility. Those with more, whether talent, education, or fortune, must give more.

It is also necessary to distinguish between authority and leadership. Every human group requires a chief, a leader. Etymologically, the word *chief* means: "Who is at the head" or, as Monsignor Tihamér Tóth said: "The one who is a head, a head that sees, thinks and acts, but for the benefit of the entire body."

Every leader needs authority and the moral or physical strength to be obeyed to perform their function. Authority is legitimized by its fundamental purpose of service, that is, seeking the well-being of subordinates and society in general.

However, we must distinguish between the boss who has control by imposition and force and the one who has control by the free choice of his associates.

The former is only a boss who will only last for a while as such, and the latter is an authentic leader.

Without leaders, society will not work; it will be chaotic. If leaders are bad, society functions poorly. If they are corrupt, society starts corrupting itself. But if leaders are healthy, strong, and competent, with a true awareness of service, society will be healthy and progressive, working in peace and harmony.

Consequently, a leader, leadership is essential in any human group. Anarchy does not work, and our deep desires for freedom must be subjected to the needs of order because otherwise, that alleged freedom turns into chaos.

However, it is necessary to recognize that these concepts of leadership, authority, order, and so on can be and are, in fact, dangerous when their application is abused or perverted, as in the following cases:

- abuse of authority turned into tyranny;
- excessive leadership, which alienates people;

- excessive order, which can lead to fascism;
- excessive freedom, which can lead to anarchy.

> In summary, leadership:
>
> - is indispensable;
> - must be healthy and be at the service of higher values;
> - must be permeated with awareness of service;
> - must respect personal freedom;
> - must be subsidiary.

CHARACTERISTICS OF A LEADER

We have discussed the nature of leadership and why it is necessary; let's now review what a leader's characteristics and qualities must be. If we tried to make a detailed list of the desirable attributes of a leader, it would be very long, and we would face the risk of forgetting some. However, if we try to list the main ones and put them in order of importance, the list will look like this:

- A leader must love fellow people. This feature would seem enough, but it is important to be more precise.
- A leader must be respectable. This would include a solid foundation of moral values.
- The leader must be persistent, and the tenacity must be accompanied by vitality, responsibility, and effective work.
- The leader must desire achievement, realization, dreams and hopes, reflection, and fundamental thought.
- The leader must have social responsibility, know social principles, and how to apply them.

○ The leader needs communication skills.
○ The leader must be cautious.
○ The leader needs to be humble.
○ The leader must have strength.

The list could go on and, hence, be somewhat unrealistic. Although it is impossible to find a human being with all these attributes, knowing what they are to promote and evaluate them is necessary. In the process of finding leaders in Grupo Bimbo, experience has taught me that the essential qualities that an actual leading manager must meet, above all else, so that their leadership turns out to be appropriate, are the eight elements listed below:

A company will be a reflection of its people, and they, in turn, will be a reflection of their leaders.

1. **Integrity.** The most important thing is to be a respectable person who respects values, is honest and faithful to their family, and does not lie.

2. **Intelligence.** The leader must have a level of intelligence appropriate for the job to be performed, with a higher potential. Intelligence that

allows understanding abstract issues, planning, organizing, and being cautious. Of course, the same level is not required for a Deputy Director as it is for a Production Supervisor.

3. **Work spirit and capacity.** We search for a person with a strong spirit to work, not a lazy or passive person, who displays strength, is not afraid of work, and is a role model in that regard. A leader must set an example.

4. **Capacity to relate to others.** We also call this characteristic *human sense*. The leader must show this ability. We do not want the leader to be a sea urchin or troublesome. Many leaders fail because they issue too many orders, try to yell orders at everyone, or do not know how to manage their associates.

5. **Leadership.** The person must have leadership skills. We used to believe that a person could lead with the previous four items checked, but we have seen that leadership is more complex over time. In Grupo Bimbo, the leader must attract, motivate and inspire the rest to do things.

6. **Profitability awareness.** The leader must be aware of the business and profitability and understand that all decisions must be made regarding a financial result at a given term. Perhaps intentions are really good, but they may be something other than profitability.

7. **Focus on results.** This requirement is related to the previous one. Focus on getting results. Get what you are looking for. Be sensitive to the difference between what adds value and what is merely functionalism.

8. **Openness to change.** We recently added this trait. In a global, accelerated business world, the dynamic of change is here to stay. The leaders and the personnel must be ready to see things differently to break paradigms.

To these eight essential qualities, I would add:

- tenacity;
- humility and austerity;
- being a team player;
- choosing and surrounding oneself with the best people;
- studying, reading, traveling;
- having a clear social conscience;
- love for people, fostering their development.

We need leaders who are prepared to face changes or, as we often say, "ready to go."

After the rigorous selection, a training process is carried out, with constant motivation, to ensure excellent leadership. If the leaders are not good, everything else becomes superfluous.

Contrary to what some may think, we are convinced that personal life cannot be separated from work life. A person is but oneself and it is not logical to believe that someone who is a liar or dishonest in their personal life will not be the same in their job.

Companies that disregard this obvious reality soon begin to pay the price, which can be cheap if the person is removed from his position or very expensive if they keep that person on, with which the organization would be steering away from its corporate mystique of attracting the best people.

Every time we compromise on these characteristics, sooner or later, we experience failure. This is where leadership gets its complicated nature, as does the responsibility that stems from it for those who exercise it and those who elect leaders.

In light of these reflections, many of us wonder, why do people elect and accept mediocre leaders?

The answer lies in what we said earlier about Ortega y Gasset's social muteness, the human phenomenon of not reacting until things become really serious. Often dazzled by luxury, pomp and promises, humankind applauds scoundrels who exploit and impoverish it.

> **Developing and Third World countries have historically been plagued by corruption, misuse of influence, credentialism, inefficiency and bureaucracy. We have not only allowed these characteristics and customs but also cheered and applauded them. Fortunately, even though this situation is changing, we all, young or old, must also take responsibility for appointing the best leaders.**

Therefore, I'm convinced that healthy leadership is essential. In any area we act in, we must be alert in choosing, appointing, accepting, and supporting only those leaders who truly meet the requirements. We must oppose undesirable people who wish to occupy those positions with all our might and possibilities.

Chapter 9
Challenges

In this chapter, I will discuss Bimbo's challenges. Although we have overcome these challenges for many years, they represent a war that may never be won for good. The need to operate more efficiently grows incessantly. *Quality*, *productivity*, and *globalization* are stories that have not ended. Just when we think they're done, a new chapter begins.

Quality demands constant evolution: developing new teams, introducing new materials, and using more nutritious raw materials.

In the Group, we have always managed to improve productivity as a team, as personnel, with distribution routes, and in sales and communications, among other areas.

But the search is endless.

PRODUCTIVITY

According to one author, productivity is infinite. Humanity, with its intelligence and will, searches for and finds ways to do things at a lower cost.

Some think productivity means working more, while others believe it's about working harder or faster. In short, they consider productivity a process that requires greater effort.

But it is not so. Productivity is quite the opposite; it means obtaining the same result with less effort, less waste, and a lower cost or achieving more with the same effort or expense.

Productivity is working with more intelligence, not with more intensity.

Productivity is found when we ask ourselves questions such as the following:

- Is everything we do necessary?
- Can it be done more simply?
- Can downtimes be eliminated?
- Is it necessary to waste so much?
- How can we save time, material, and energy?
- Can a manual process be mechanized?

Productivity is the factor that contributes the most to improving people's quality of life. Each person's contribution to productivity may help many, perhaps for several generations.

Apparent work

It is important to differentiate among the diverse kinds of work to distinguish the sectors that really produce and the sectors that only appear to work:

- In the *primary sector,* people work in agriculture, livestock, mining, forestry, fishing activities, and some agribusiness processes.
- In the *secondary sector,* people work on activities transforming durable or consumer goods. This covers industrial activities.
- In the *tertiary sector,* people provide services to society, such as transportation, commerce, communications, hotels, tourism, education, entertainment, culture, public services, etc.

These are the three productive sectors.

Unfortunately, there is also a *quaternary sector* that produces nothing, provides no service, and does not contribute to society in any way. We must view with disbelief those who take shelter under the apparent mantle of work but who actually do not contribute to the hard collective effort.

Reasonable productivity

Why insist on the issue of productivity? Simply because we still need to reach reasonable productivity.

We could say that productivity is equivalent to the quantity and quality of the results obtained from a job.

Remuneration for this work is, or should be, a direct ratio of productivity. If little is produced, remuneration cannot be high. This is precisely the problem of developing countries.

That is why we urge people to work more productively. We should not have jobs that do not produce or produce very little. We must ensure that each position becomes more productive and thus can be better paid. Together, we must find ways to do things more productively.

PRODUCTIVITY AND AUSTERITY

In the situation that our countries are currently experiencing, more than ever, productivity and austerity are undoubtedly the concepts that should inspire the standard of living of all citizens. Everyone must produce more, work better, figure things out, risk a lot, and organize intelligently. All countries, but especially those at the lowest level of development, need the best efforts from all their men.

We also need to be austere in our spending. Governments, institutions, companies, groups, and families must do without what is unnecessary, avoiding squandering and waste at all costs. As individuals, caution advises us to save to prevent future problems and invest wisely if there is a surplus.

We are facing a historical dilemma: either every one of us does something about it today, or in the near future, we will witness our failure and disappointment.

Productivity, the engine of modern life

Indeed, productivity is the driving force of modern life. If production processes were frozen in their current state, the entire world would face a crisis with unimaginable consequences. Therefore, I consider it essential to maintain the pace of progress that new generations expect and increase productivity correspondingly.

Experience shows that it is increasingly easier to do things with less effort, with fewer resources and in less time, i.e., with greater productivity. In other words, we can achieve more with the same or fewer resources.

Entrepreneurs of any level must be persistently concerned with and unquestionably devoted to constantly achieving greater productivity. They cannot be content, as they were for several centuries, with doing things as they have always been done.

A country's wealth is not measured by its natural resources but by the productivity of its people.

Personal productivity is measured by the added value that is finally obtained. Although it is undeniable that this productivity depends mainly on the appropriate use of capital goods, the careful and professional analysis of each function is required to get each person to work, not more intensely, but more intelligently.

This analysis, adaptation and reordering will only be achieved if top managers decide to do it and if this decision is supported and implemented.

Obviously, this goal of productivity must allow for better pay for the associate, which will be the start of a virtuous circle:

A large portion of the value of the United States-Mexico-Canada Agreement (USMCA) lies in this concept.

Underdevelopment persists because people's low purchasing power is due to low productivity, which stems from poor work organization.

I am referring to the need for anyone who performs a job, whatever it may be, to do so efficiently and effectively, using equipment that maximizes productivity.

What is truly tragic is that the explainable problem of the impossibility of poor societies to provide costly equipment of capital goods to associates is combined with the lack of systems and, above all, the lack of an attitude that seeks and procures personal productivity.

This can be described as an underdeveloped culture that prevails in Third World countries. Personal work is generally unproductive, and the lack of planning is compensated for with more labor. Another vicious circle appears: pay is bad because employees are inefficient, and they are inefficient because they are paid little. This situation is exemplified by that popular but terrible phrase: "One pretends to pay, and the other pretends to work."

In my long history of business activity, I have become convinced that entrepreneurs are responsible for the good and the bad, for what is done and what is not done, for growth, technological change or stagnation and obsolescence; that is, the responsibility lies in the hands of the head who leads the company, makes the final decisions and assumes the risk.

In his marvelous book *A New Entrepreneur Spirit*, Lawrence M. Miller states that no worthwhile change can be achieved without a strong official's energetic and tenacious leadership at the highest level.

The business leader must understand the need for work to be organized in a highly productive way. The associate cannot decide this; it is the leader's social responsibility. The entrepreneur will determine the effectiveness of the position and its pay, the company's competitiveness, the country's competitiveness and, ultimately, the population's standard of living.

Personal productivity

Another critical aspect is personal productivity. Not long ago, I read a phrase that completes this thought: "People are the true wealth of a nation when they have been taught to fight for life, to work and to produce."

Of course, they must be provided with the material resources to do so. Anyone transporting firewood needs a trailer, which costs hundreds of thousands of dollars. Economic resources are essential for productivity.

However, in countries that are not making progress, in addition to needing more resources, they also need the mindset. The leader is the one who needs to say that it is not necessary to have six people to distribute ice; two can do the job with systems, methods, tools, motivation, and better pay (this way, they will earn more and will be able to spend money that will generate jobs for other people). If this is not done in this manner, the only thing achieved is increasing misery.

For example, years ago, in the question and answers section after a conference, someone jumped up and said: "Hey, what you say is immoral because if to have productivity you have to replace people with machines, what are they going to do after they are left unemployed?" I replied: "What is being proposed here is not to take away a person's job. The proposal is to make that job more productive. If, instead of working with 10 or 20 mule drivers and ten donkeys, I do it with a truck driver and a truck, I am giving work to those who design that truck, to those who produce it, to those who give maintenance to the truck and all those people earn more than those who drive the donkeys. So, if I give work to those who design, build, maintain, produce gasoline, make tires, I think I am generating better-paid employment for many people."

As we said, this productivity largely depends on the appropriate use of capital goods. However, while we must make the greatest effort to become more technical and modernize equipment, as well as provide associates with the production means and jobs to allow them to be more efficient, we must also become aware that, even without the addition of capital goods, there are enormous possibilities to make personal work more productive.

Years ago, trucks drove down the streets delivering ice in Mexico, and five or six youngsters rode on them. How much could they make? If we consider the low price of ice, the driver's pay, the cost of the truck and the other guys, we see that there was no productivity; they were deceiving themselves.

We see another example of this at gas stations, although less than before, where the drivers arrive at the station and eight or ten people are fighting to serve them, making it very clear that the productivity of those workers is null. This does not happen in France, Germany, the United States or Canada, where drivers load gasoline into their cars. The cashier at gas stations in France or the United States, where cars arrive and drivers fill their tanks and pay on their own, enjoys the opportunity to produce more. If there is no productivity, there can be no wealth or, obviously, distribution of wealth.

Productivity is the only thing that allows a country to develop, grow, educate, and progress. Hence, everyone needs to be aware of the need to be productive.

A commission from the Massachusetts Institute of Technology (MIT), formed in the late 1980s to investigate industrial productivity of the United States, establishes in its conclusions: "American industry displays worrying signs of weakness, and in many sectors of the economy, shows that companies in the United States are losing ground to their overseas competitors [...] that these disorders are not ups and downs of a normal process, but rather symptoms of a generalized disease."

They also report that this situation will not be corrected by making greater and better efforts with the same tactics as in the recent past. The international environment has changed irrevocably, and the United States must adapt its practices to this new world.

If this happens to the country that has been the leader of the First World, what can those of us living in less developed countries expect?

Now, regarding productivity, awareness of optimizing resources and the ability to organize them effectively and efficiently play essential roles.

As explained previously, this analysis, adaptation and reordering work will only occur if top management executives decide to do it and if this decision is supported and implemented.

It is evident that a wealthy society can provide its associates with equipment and facilities that allow them to be highly productive.

When you obtain both a high investment per individual and the mindset and organization for productivity, you achieve an impressive level of efficiency that would otherwise be impossible to achieve.

When we hear assertions that "increasing productivity in all economic activity is an essential condition to achieving real wage increases and to strengthening the nation's economy," we all agree. But the truth is that our culture keeps dragging us down. It continues operating inefficiently and, consequently, with barely sufficient salaries to survive.

What matters here is to become aware that this cultural change is essential because it has no substitute. It is urgent because social demands and the fair aspirations of people for a worthy life cannot wait much longer.

This cultural change can only be induced by social leaders linked to the productive sphere, that is, businesspeople, who have the possibility, responsibility and opportunity to induce and promote this cultural change.

The issue of productivity has been a core concern in my professional life because I believe that the success and survival of any company depend on the ability of its managers to constantly achieve higher productivity levels.

PRODUCTIVITY IN A GLOBAL ECONOMY

1. The increase in productivity in the globalization era depends on companies' compliance with the requirements listed and explained below.

It is a well-known fact that the ability to generate wealth or personal productivity is directly related to a person's **level of education and training.**

With due exceptions in both senses, those with the highest levels of education obtain the highest income and create the greatest wealth.

Therefore, the first step to increasing productivity, although this does not have short-term effects, is strongly boosting education. There are no shortcuts or alternatives.

We must raise the level of education, mainly for the majority. More and better schooling is required. Without this, there would be no significant progress.

Lack of education produces poverty, dissatisfaction, and frustration and compromises social peace. Every one of us who plays some leadership role in the country must make a great and continued effort to advance in educational matters.

Although this effort is understood as a quantitative and qualitative improvement in education, a new approach is also required in higher education.

Only some people can or must pursue a university degree; therefore, as in other countries, professional, technological or trade careers must be promoted, and people should be allowed to study them. People with good technical training are much more productive and accomplished than university students who cannot find a spot in the market.

It should be noted that the huge education gap can be quickly reduced if we learn to use virtual communication tools offered by new technologies.

2. Another requirement for increasing productivity is the **economic resources to obtain capital goods,** which makes the production of goods and services more efficient.

Capital goods require money or adequate financing. Ideally, this should come from internal savings or reasonable-cost credits.

It is obvious that, without capital goods, it is almost impossible to compete in a global economy.

Many of our countries' problems result from our inability to make the necessary transition to compete in a global economy. We had to stay current with new technologies, do our research and development as much as possible, provide staff training, mechanize, automate, and further utilize the advantages of information technology and computer science.

Yes, this requires capital, which has been scarce and expensive in many countries. However, not all problems stem from a lack of resources; in many cases, there was apathy, a lack of vision and an unquestioned habit of milking companies for personal expenses instead of reinvesting.

Productivity demands fresh resources, and all responsible businesspeople must fulfill this task.

Poor countries face the dilemma of needing more resources; therefore, promoting domestic savings must be a first-order task, and this is not only the responsibility of the government but also of all citizens.

The only benefit of crises is that they force us to think and rectify many things. Faced with the impossibility of procuring capital resources due to a lack of money or cheap credit, some have tried to export and obtain financing at international rates. It is actually exciting to see how people's needs sharpen the genius of those who are unsatisfied with regrets and blaming others but who make an effort and move forward.

As a final comment on capital goods, in countries that offer cheap labor, there may be a temptation to do without truly efficient equipment. This leads to maintaining the vicious circle of inefficient work, poor pay, and depressed consumption.

3. An additional requirement for capital goods is **to obtain and apply the most appropriate technologies.**

In some cases, cutting-edge technology, not even the most advanced, will not be necessary. However, in general, the most modern technologies are the most efficient.

The economic resource requirement we discussed previously precisely focuses on access to industrial processing information and administrative technologies. A modern company of any type lives in an environment where change and the speed with which it occurs are already primordial elements for strategic planning and administrative processes.

Conforming to change and using more sophisticated tools, such as total quality, reengineering, and other programs or methodologies, is indispensable for the development and survival of organizations.

This is not the space to delve into such an important topic, but it is proven that simplifying processes is essential in the logical and necessary search for productivity. However, the massive dismissal of excess personnel is not the answer. There are intelligent mechanisms to do this without losing the personnel's talent or motivation and, very importantly, without creating a social problem.

4. Finally, another indispensable requirement for productivity is **personnel involvement and the establishment of a harmonious and enthusiastic relationship** in the productive center.

The workforce must perceive that they are working towards a common objective, that expectations are convergent, and that an environment of fairness, trust, care, and equitable benefit distribution prevails.

There will always be differences and tensions in labor relations. Still, there is a big difference between companies that genuinely respect their personnel and want their involvement and fulfillment as people and those that only use and manipulate them.

There are countries and companies with all the technological, financial, and administrative resources. Still, they cannot attain the efficiency and productivity they desire because they maintain an adversarial, absurd relationship from a social point of view, eventually becoming an obstacle to achieving their goals.

In my opinion, the *Japanese miracle*, and in fact that of the other Asian countries, is due above all to the climate of involvement, the sense of mission and the coincidence of objectives of all those who work in a given company. The problem of Western companies is not necessarily the adversarial relationship but simple disinterest and bureaucracy, which marginalizes their members due to the companies' shortsightedness, frustrating them and wasting their potential.

It would be impossible to determine which of the above requirements is the most important for achieving the much-needed productivity. However, I believe all four are essential, and addressing them will yield the expected short—or long-term results.

Nonetheless, the last one—which includes the importance of the company having a philosophy, a code of ethics, an attitude it wishes to see and encourages in everyone, and I emphasize, not only in a few but every individual who is a part of said company, with their genuine engagement in the activity that is being carried out—is not just indispensable in obtaining results, but for strengthening, at the same time, the system and guaranteeing social development and peace.

GLOBALIZATION

Only a few years ago, developing countries began participating in globalization. We do not know whether they will end up with three large commercial blocks, one large commercial block, regional blocks, or once more isolated countries. However, globalization entails a critical challenge for all companies today and for several years to come.

I see globalization in a very personal way. It has existed since the beginning of humankind, allowing humans to relate to one another and exchange information and goods. As communication media evolved, people left their communities and started exchanging merchandise.

This process has accelerated dramatically in recent years due to the development of mass media.

The minute the media, particularly the Internet, became a part of life, they influenced human communication as distances disappeared, including the costs they represent.

If China can produce the tail of a 747 plane cheaper than they can do it in the United States, or if Mexico can make a telephone more affordable than in Germany, it is evident that business will start to be carried out in that fashion. It is inevitable and positive, but it needs to be regulated and understood. It requires that the most powerful (countries, societies, companies, people) consider its possible effects on the less powerful. Great social responsibility must be shown in that sense. For example, Hong Kong has an awesome tourist infrastructure and offers labor for one dollar per day. And that's only in Hong Kong, let alone China. It is unfair, I would even say immoral, for one to take advantage of that labor.

Those are the aspects that must be attended to in globalization. If the approach is that money is the only thing that matters, all these issues become an actual aggression on society. This is where anti-globalization and other protest groups originate. The former are right in certain things but at the wrong extreme. I think that globalization is positive and responds to the value of human solidarity. If I can enjoy a better butter made in Belgium at a reasonable price and the Belgians drink tequila produced in Mexico, that would be great; we both win. However, goodwill and the establishment of standards are needed so that globalization does not become an aggressive and abusive process.

How we insert ourselves into globalization

Although our original intention was only to export, two types of situations started in time: offerings for us to buy companies and acquisition offerings or partnerships with transnational companies. Upon exploring the offers to purchase companies, we saw some quite viable opportunities and synergies. The offers to acquire or partner with large transnational food product companies through investment banking representatives were constant. As we have never considered selling the Group, we thought that one way to avoid being absorbed by those giants was to become a company with a presence abroad.

We can also consider exporting our business philosophy when considering investments outside of our country.

Our fundamental objective is to create highly productive and deeply humane companies. Although we have yet to fully attain either of these objectives, we are deeply satisfied with our continued efforts.

The role played by our diplomatic representation in the various countries where we operate can be helpful for Mexican companies that wish to internationalize.

Our Group, in particular, has received invaluable help from ambassadors and other diplomats. They have guided, accompanied, or even introduced us to the authorities and helped with complicated procedures such as trademark registrations, among other things.

It is motivating to watch our representatives' efforts in organizing flea markets, dinners, cocktails, and other activities to support and promote Mexican initiatives. We are pleased and grateful that links with local importers are promoted and that we are invited as potential investors. This proactive activity, which benefits Mexico's development, is highly productive.

POINTS TO CONSIDER REGARDING INTERNATIONALIZATION

During our incursions into different countries, we gained some experience, which is important to summarize and share. Among the main points that should be considered when starting the internationalization process are the following:

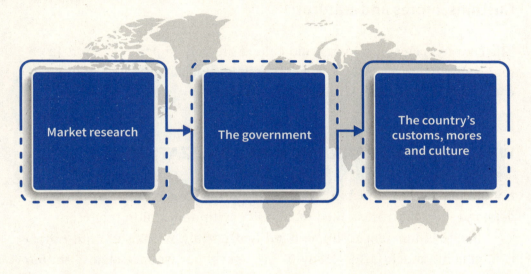

Market research

When we start operations in a new country, we conduct market research to help us understand the local population's consumption patterns. When this research is not professional, careful, and responsible, it sometimes leads us to believe certain products would sell well. Nevertheless, when produced in our bakery in the target country, they did not sell or sell less than projected.

Even though proper market research is a valuable tool for entering new markets, more information is required to adjust to the actual demand conditions.

The government

The government is a decisive factor when entering a new country. We have received great support from the governments of the different countries where we work. Governments that support companies help their country grow.

Customs, mores and culture

The country's customs, mores and culture are very important factors in entering a new market. People have different customs, ways of calling things, eating habits, meal times, and flavors and tastes.

WHAT WE CAN LEARN FROM GLOBALIZATION

My opinion is that globalization is an important concept that we must understand, become accustomed to, and live with now and in the future.

Change is inherent to humankind and has always existed, but now it is happening much faster. Many of the issues that we face stem from our resistance to change, from our clinging to what we know because it gives us comfort and confidence, but only those who know how to face that challenge move forward at its pace instead of being dragged by it.

Our younger leaders believed that we had the capacity to be one of the largest baking companies in the world. Today, we are. I have been asked, for example, in Argentina: "And why do you come here? What can you contribute?" My answer is: "We can contribute valuable things. In merely operational, economic terms, I believe we can contribute with technology, quality, service, and new products." We have automated the production of various products with machinery that does not exist in other parts of the world and which we had to develop. Today, these lines are worth two and three million dollars each, and we are proud of them because we have designed them. In the past, everything was done by hand.

Yes, we provide technology, good products, and systems. Everyone has their own values throughout our distribution system, as does our marketing strategy.

On the other hand, we can also contribute to the crucial human and social aspects. When we took over the bakery we bought in Guatemala, the associates told us, "They had never spoken to us like this, they had never taken us into account like this, they had never respected us like this."

For this reason, we are confident in our knowledge and expertise regarding economic, technological, and administrative fields, as well as the human, social and values-related aspects.

In this respect, many interesting anecdotes arise in our daily jobs. For example, one day, an associate retiring and his wife visited me. When I inquired about their visit, they said: "We came to thank you." I replied, "Thank me? There is nothing to be thankful for; you worked; I am the one who should thank you." "Look," he replied, "if it hadn't been for Bimbo, my life would be different. I still live with the same woman…" It is satisfying to see that there are families who feel and recognize that their lives would have been different if they had not worked with us.

A first lesson regarding globalization is that change is inevitable; it has its reason for existing, and it is precisely by changing for the better that companies and people can advance, with caution, to the forefront.

In Latin America, we hear news about bankruptcies, closures, and failures daily, especially among small and medium-sized companies. Although it is regrettable, we must analyze whether the root of the problem they face is not having adapted to the new circumstances, not having modernized, not having acquired new technologies, not having trained the personnel, etc. In short, it would be helpful to find out if, facing a profound change at the global and national level, their administrators continued doing things in the same manner, that is, as some people say, they continued *milking* the companies instead of reinvesting in them or reconverting them.

The second lesson is that the company must transform itself economically and socially. Economically, it must move closer to international technological levels. Like us, countries that have opened to globalization no longer constitute protected economies, as we did until a few years ago. We face competition from all around the world, with robotic systems, equipment, processes, and computer systems, as well as important innovations resulting from intensive research and development programs stemming from the need for survival in a very competitive environment.

It is clear that we cannot continue operating with backward technologies or obsolete and inefficient equipment because doing so guarantees our decline and eventual disappearance. *Reconversion* has become a requirement. It is appropriate to remember the phrase "Renew or die." This is an opportunity to prepare for companies in countries that have not yet reached international-level competition.

A company cannot hope to be global without adapting to all these aspects. Transferring successful models to other countries is difficult; many unforeseen issues crop up everywhere. But if, on top of it all, we only have an upgrading system within the usual, entering globalization will be a much more difficult task.

The third lesson is to learn, listen and seek ways to complement each other. Knowing the diversity of cultures, tastes and systems allows us to compete with other countries and benefit mutually.

We acquired a very solid company in the United States. We realized that we could benefit from what they had learned throughout their successful history, especially in terms of product quality, the relationship with supermarket chains and industrial safety. They, in turn, were excited to learn about our bakeries and our strong presence in the market.

It is very satisfying to observe the enthusiastic participation of people from various companies and countries in several of our operations or corporate meetings, who are now focused on one common and complementary objective.

Conclusions about our responsibility as entrepreneurs, given globalization

1. Despite their recognized benefits, free market systems have yet to close the gap between the rich and the poor, especially recently. This happens as much in countries as it does in people.
2. If businesspeople in the globalized world fail to realize that we have a social responsibility that goes hand in hand with our economic duties, we will place humankind at a considerable risk.
3. The free-market system can be the path to achieving a better world as long as it operates with social responsibility and its purely liberal conception is eliminated.
4. Globalization is parallel to human solidarity and is inevitable. We must channel it well.
5. Entrepreneurs have the most significant responsibility for this process to be fair and for the benefit of all, not just for some.

OUTSTANDING CHALLENGES FOR GRUPO BIMBO

Currently, the Group is facing several challenges, among them those listed below:

- The main challenge is finding more efficient and less expensive ways of working and producing, as there is currently a global effort to lower costs.
- Another challenge is the changing market. In the past, our customers were small; now, the trend is towards large store chains. This implies a different way of working.
- Another challenge is our national and international competitors.
- We also face the challenge of being creative, looking for new products, and finding better solutions to people's needs and society's general needs.

OUTSTANDING CHALLENGES FOR DEVELOPING AND THIRD WORLD COUNTRIES

Developing and Third World countries face specific challenges, for instance:

- The biggest challenge these countries face is understanding that we must embrace change, which implies, above all, ending corruption and inefficient, unproductive work.

We missed a golden opportunity to fix essential things in these countries. When corruption ends or is reduced, when bureaucracy (understood as part of the non-producing sector) decreases, we must start making all necessary changes and adjustments to invest there.

In terms of infrastructure, for example, we need ports, airports, highways, and roads; we must work to improve fishing, agriculture, forestry, and tourism.

Yes, everything needs to be done in this group of countries. We have the leadership, but the chaos of unproductivity, bureaucracy and corruption still embedded in them does not allow progress.

- Another challenge: it is essential to try to attain national unity in every country, as well as fostering dialogue, rapprochement, and support between nations.

Chapter 10
Some personal ideas

Our responsibility in all prevailing economic activities is strongly conditioned by the characteristics of the regime in which we operate.

Roberto Servitje

THE COUNTRY THAT WE WANT

Developing and Third World countries are neither more nor less than what their citizens are. We are the architects of the good and evil in our countries. We cannot criticize them without criticizing ourselves. We cannot blame anyone for our problems and failures.

If we want better countries, we must work for them; nobody will do it for us. We and our ancestors have shaped our countries throughout time, and we can continue doing so with effort, hard work, and respect for our values.

Our traditions, governments, and countries will be what we want them to be!

THE VOTE

Living in society demands that we all contribute and are aware of our rights and obligations. Fulfilling these obligations is the only way to make social life possible.

Our laws embody our right to choose those we consider suitable to rule over us: our right to vote. Nonetheless, voting is not only our right but also our obligation.

Some people do not vote because they do not understand the enormous importance of the election of a ruler for them and their loved ones. They don't vote because they think that doing so or refusing to do so changes nothing. That attitude is wrong: voting should be one of the primary obligations of an adult.

We must understand the political process more deeply, know the parties, their candidates, and their tendencies, and vote for those who best represent all social sectors throughout our country.

This is why it is important for every responsible citizen to be aware of politics. As a renowned French author once said, getting involved in politics is what really matters; it is assuming our responsibility to the extent that it pertains to each of us.

Undoubtedly, without the complete participation of citizens, there cannot be a good government. Even though we assume that we choose the best to rule our country, citizens need to give leaders feedback so that they fulfill their duties in the interests of all of society.

> **Entrepreneurs are part of society and its economy, but the proper operation of our companies is strongly conditioned by the characteristics of the regime in which we operate. Therefore, we need a suitable government framework for our companies to be healthy.**

Logical laws are required worldwide to encourage investment, employment, job creation, and productivity and to allow international competitiveness. However, we are still far from that scenario.

In some countries, consumer taxes are a serious problem. As the middle class has decreased dramatically, this tax significantly impacts the less favored classes. This is why finding a smart solution that promotes productivity and job creation is necessary. Laws must change.

On the other hand, many countries are saturated with red tape, partly because of the corruption we have discussed. This kind of cancer affects the economy in two ways: it promotes business development outside the law and slows down the development of companies that actually comply with the law, stimulating activities that are not regulated.

At any given moment, government corruption permeates down to people offering public services who ask for a *little help* or things like that.

This does not happen in Europe, where entrepreneurs from several countries that have entered the European Union, such as Spain, Greece, and Portugal, have managed to develop their companies and contributed to their countries' advancement thanks to an enormous housing effort. These companies provide employment, use local materials, and generate huge psychological satisfaction in their associates.

There has been a huge housing boom in Spain, Portugal, and Greece. Thousands of condominiums have been built, which has boosted the economy.

What happens in developing countries? There is a considerable need for housing, and we have all the necessary material resources. We do not have to import anything and have plenty of labor.

In the last century, imperfect systems had valuable principles but lacked other elementary ones, leading to failure. Dazzled by their apparent logic, they searched for an ideal society, placing pieces like puzzle pieces in which everything seemed to fit together except for the last piece.

Different social systems, adopted and driven by Eastern and Western countries, faced problems and failed for the same fundamental reason: they did not respect the dignity of the people.

This makes it evident that our main concern right now must be finding an economic system that is better than those implemented in the past, one that is good not only for some or for most but for all. A good system should differ from the puzzle we mentioned, in which almost all the elements fit together, but some do not. This would show that something is not right and be a symptom that one of the great social principles has been violated.

It is time for people to learn those lessons and choose and demand the government they need. It is everyone's responsibility, but perhaps now more so the responsibility of young people, to ensure and fight for their representatives to propose, embody, and support a government structure based on the highest values and social principles.

There is a saying that people have the governments they deserve, and that is true. We all raise our voices against failures, inefficiencies, abuses, and corruption, but we do not take a minute to reflect on the fact that we are all involved. We have a lot to do to improve the situation.

Corruption is a transcendental aspect of this. When it permeates all everyday life activities, it distorts everything, making it impossible to aim for order and legality.

After a brief analysis, we can see that many of our problems stem from the corruption of those who offer and accept bribes: a lack of parking, pollution, insecurity and crime, poor infrastructure, etc.

Data issued by the World Bank show that during the last four decades of the past century, many developing countries progressed at an incredible rate, both in health and education. In economics, some quintupled their average income at an unprecedented rate in history.

The upheavals of the last decade painted a less optimistic picture. Still, the growth of the past decades indicates that the dream of rapid and sustained development can become a reality.

If we long for a better world—and we certainly do—we must do whatever is necessary to change this culture. While the average citizen can only do little to achieve a proper government framework, he can do much more in the socio-economic sphere.

Virtually every citizen is both the subject and the object of economic activity. The sum of our actions and omissions influences the different areas of social activity. Direct results may be observed in every country's financial, cultural, artistic, and ecological order and other aspects of people's lives.

Thus, if we wish to achieve the progress we have mentioned, we must improve many, if not all, of the cells that make up the social fabric. We must implement important changes if we want the total to yield better results comparable to those of developed societies.

Finally, the family is society's fundamental cell, and healthy family integration is vital for healthy social development. Hence, preserving an atmosphere of affection, respect, and solidarity in the family is indispensable for building a balanced society.

Another such cell is the school, which is responsible for providing the education on which people's livelihoods and development depend. Therefore, governments must understand that education is a priority above many others and that all the efforts and sacrifices made to move decisively towards higher levels of education will never suffice.

International institutions responsible for promoting social development attribute a decisive role to education, particularly elementary school. Therefore, it is essential that we first understand our educational system and then support its continuous improvement with all our might.

We must make a considerable effort to ensure that education imparts knowledge and conveys spiritual values and moral principles. Mikhail Gorbachev[†], whom I admired and respected, wrote in his book *Perestroika* that "currently, our main job is to elevate every person spiritually, respecting their inner world and strengthening their morality."

I want to think that very few people of this generation have lived experiences as intense as his; therefore, they have not had to think, meditate, and assess alternatives as he has. When he points out the latter, it is because he considers this is how the root of the social problems that bring about social unrest in the modern world may be tackled.

We entrepreneurs offer everything we can to society. We are its workhorses. We want to be fed and treated well, but we also search for productivity, employment, and technology. We are those who produce and on whom a country's economic and social development largely depends.

Obviously, we must also pay taxes, be respectful, comply with environmental regulations, and, in short, be responsible. For this purpose, we need encouragement and support. Countries where entrepreneurs are supported, such as Singapore, a small island without resources, have emerged with one of the most thriving economies in the world. The country's per capita income is impressive, and this is because its government encourages and supports all entrepreneurial work.

Because I am a businessperson, and because I am sure that many of the readers of this book are or will be, and because in one way or another, we all have a relationship with companies, in the following table, I present a broader outline of the companies' transcendent function, their responsibility and how they can adapt to better play the role that they play in society.

- Companies—and I maintain this in all forums because it seems necessary that they are understood thus—are vital institutions for life in society; without them, society could not exist as we conceive it.
- Companies are, without a doubt, the engine that moves an economy. They are the leading promoters of technology and training, the creators of employment, and the wealth generators.
- Companies are decisive in determining a nation's lifestyle and are most responsible for its living conditions. I quote Peter Drucker's approach: "Inasmuch as the problems of the company are solved, the problems of society will be solved."

At the beginning of the book, I stated that leaders must take the initiative. And here is a very important one: promoting a *sustainable society and growth*. We, who either already are or will become part of that leadership, must study the problem of achieving such a society, understand its severity, and act accordingly.

In the new environment, only those companies that understand that they have the strength to achieve that goal will be able to operate successfully.

> There is no mystery: the company that responds intelligently to social challenges, the one that serves everyone well—those on the outside (consumers), those on the inside (associates), and society as a whole—by producing wealth, caring for the environment, respecting laws, and contributing to the common good, will have secured the success it deserves.

TO UNITE OR TO SEPARATE

Throughout history, science and technology have achieved impressive feats. Suffice it to observe the technological wonders of our daily lives.

But while we have progressed by leaps and bounds in many areas, we have been stagnant in others, and it even seems that we have retreated. Humankind has wasted itself in useless wars, fratricidal revolutions and sterile confrontations, which have weakened countries and their populations alike.

If we were coherent when we stated that humankind occupies the topmost position in our scale of values, we would have to foster a climate of care, support, mutual help, and solidarity. This environment would allow human beings and governments to help each other overcome their shortcomings, exchange surpluses, provide support, and undertake united and concerted actions to achieve their development and integration and ensure people's fulfillment and happiness.

A wise recommendation states: "We must pay further attention to those elements which unite us and less to those which divide and distance us."

We must make an effort to be willing to dialogue, open to listening and strive for reconciliation because we all have the responsibility to promote peace.

History has proven that massive social uprisings occur when humanity cannot find a way to satisfy its different needs and that humanity's constant tensions and conflicts are due to injustice, inequality, abuse, marginalization, oppression, and the lack of freedom and opportunities, so there is no doubt that if we want to keep peace, we must transform our policies and our institutions so that they better respond to the great desires and needs of human beings.

Governments must be open to democracy and citizens' healthy participation. They must also be transparent and honest and fight corruption, bureaucracy and inefficiency. They must also surround themselves with the best, most capable people aware of social problems and the solutions they require.

The term *aristocracy*, discredited and prostituted by historical experiences, is still quite valid and acceptable when it is applied to refer to the government exercised by the best.

What characteristics distinguish the best leaders? They are healthy and honest rulers with ideals, vision, and strength, capable of making decisions even if they have to challenge the *status quo* and face pressures and inertia.

Appendix 1
Chronology of bakeries and plants

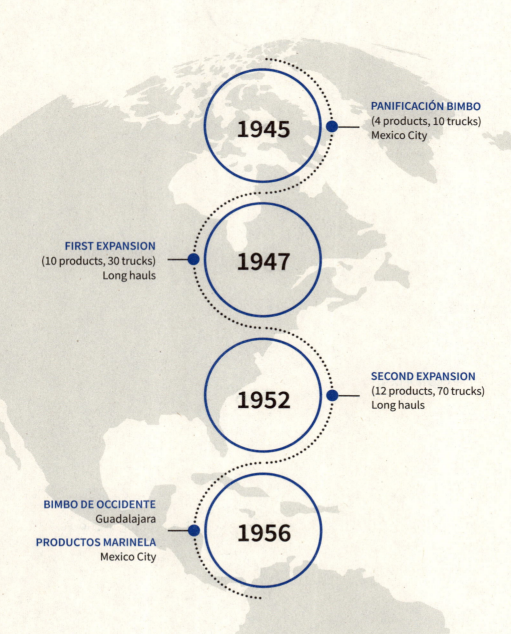

198 Bimbo. A Strategy for Corporate Success

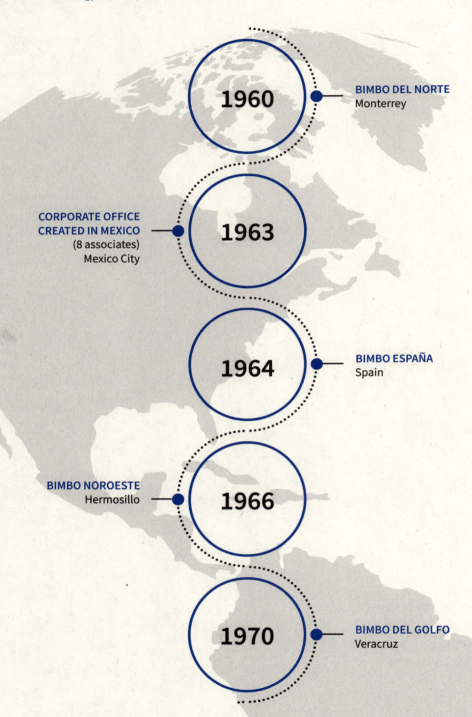

Chronology of plants 199

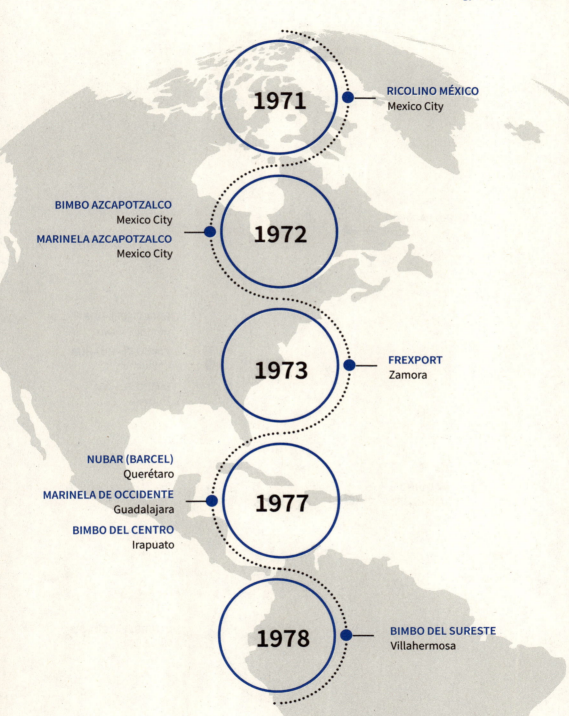

200 Bimbo. A Strategy for Corporate Success

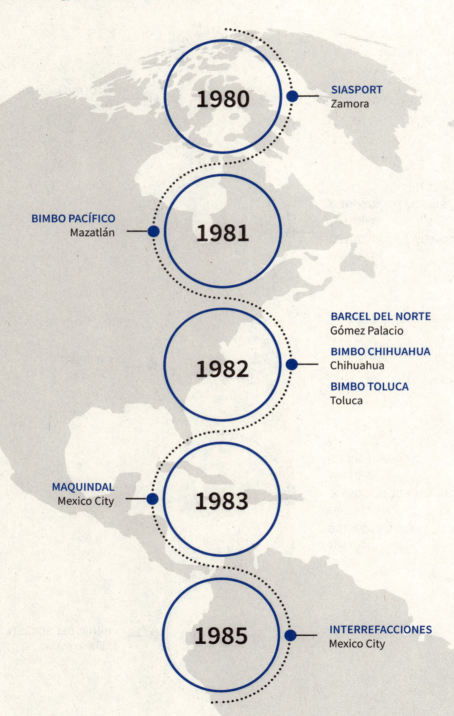

Chronology of plants 201

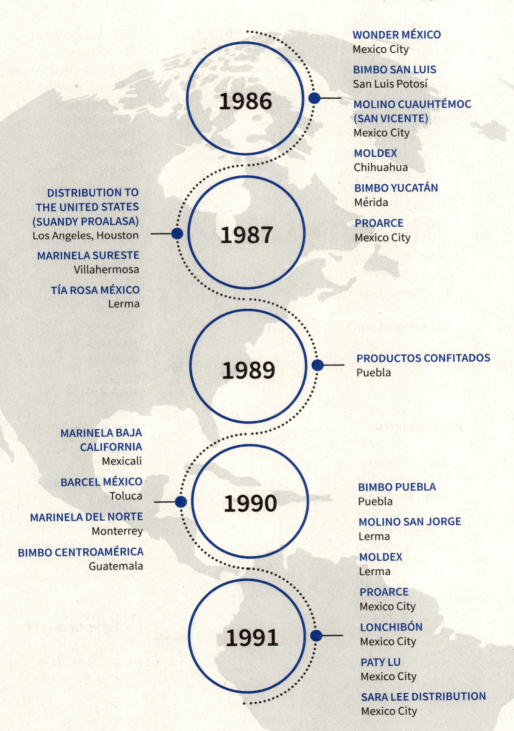

1986
- WONDER MÉXICO — Mexico City
- BIMBO SAN LUIS — San Luis Potosí
- MOLINO CUAUHTÉMOC (SAN VICENTE) — Mexico City
- MOLDEX — Chihuahua

1987
- BIMBO YUCATÁN — Mérida
- PROARCE — Mexico City
- DISTRIBUTION TO THE UNITED STATES (SUANDY PROALASA) — Los Angeles, Houston
- MARINELA SURESTE — Villahermosa
- TÍA ROSA MÉXICO — Lerma

1989
- PRODUCTOS CONFITADOS — Puebla

1990
- MARINELA BAJA CALIFORNIA — Mexicali
- BARCEL MÉXICO — Toluca
- MARINELA DEL NORTE — Monterrey
- BIMBO CENTROAMÉRICA — Guatemala
- BIMBO PUEBLA — Puebla
- MOLINO SAN JORGE — Lerma
- MOLDEX — Lerma

1991
- PROARCE — Mexico City
- LONCHIBÓN — Mexico City
- PATY LU — Mexico City
- SARA LEE DISTRIBUTION — Mexico City

202 Bimbo. A Strategy for Corporate Success

1992
- INDUSTRIAL DE MAÍZ — State of Mexico
- GALLETAS Y PASTAS LARA — Mexico City and Puebla
- BIMBO DE BAJA CALIFORNIA — Mexicali

1993
- BIMBO EL SALVADOR — El Salvador
- DICAM — State of Mexico
- AUTOVEND — Mexico City
- RICOLINO SAN LUIS — San Luis Potosí
- HOLSUM VENEZOLANA — Venezuela
- BIMAR FOODS — USA
- LA FRONTERIZA — USA
- BARCEL CHILE — Santiago de Chile
- MOLINO MONTSERRAT (Flour mill) — Veracruz
- MARINELA VENEZUELA — Venezuela

1994
- GRISSINI — Guadalajara
- MARILARA — Guadalajara
- SUANDY — State of Mexico
- FRISER — State of Mexico
- FABILA — USA
- BIMBO COSTA RICA — Costa Rica

1995
- IDEAL (BIMBO CHILE) — Chile
- BIMBO ARGENTINA — Argentina
- BIMBO HONDURAS — Honduras
- PRODUCTOS DE LECHE CORONADO — San Luis Potosí
- C & C — USA
- LA TAPATÍA — USA

1996
- PACIFIC PRIDE BAKERY — USA
- BIMBO COLOMBIA — Colombia

Chronology of plants 203

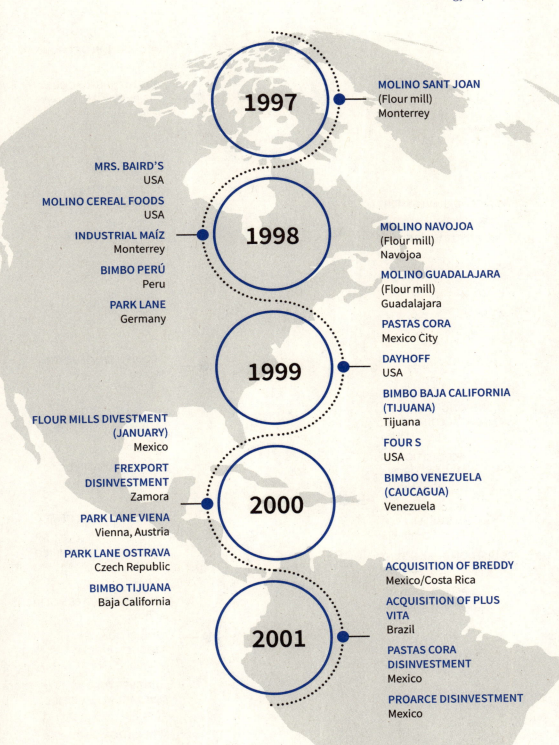

1997
- MOLINO SANT JOAN (Flour mill) Monterrey

1998
- MRS. BAIRD'S USA
- MOLINO CEREAL FOODS USA
- INDUSTRIAL MAÍZ Monterrey
- BIMBO PERÚ Peru
- PARK LANE Germany
- MOLINO NAVOJOA (Flour mill) Navojoa
- MOLINO GUADALAJARA (Flour mill) Guadalajara

1999
- PASTAS CORA Mexico City
- DAYHOFF USA
- BIMBO BAJA CALIFORNIA (TIJUANA) Tijuana

2000
- FLOUR MILLS DIVESTMENT (JANUARY) Mexico
- FREXPORT DISINVESTMENT Zamora
- PARK LANE VIENA Vienna, Austria
- PARK LANE OSTRAVA Czech Republic
- BIMBO TIJUANA Baja California
- FOUR S USA
- BIMBO VENEZUELA (CAUCAGUA) Venezuela

2001
- ACQUISITION OF BREDDY Mexico/Costa Rica
- ACQUISITION OF PLUS VITA Brazil
- PASTAS CORA DISINVESTMENT Mexico
- PROARCE DISINVESTMENT Mexico

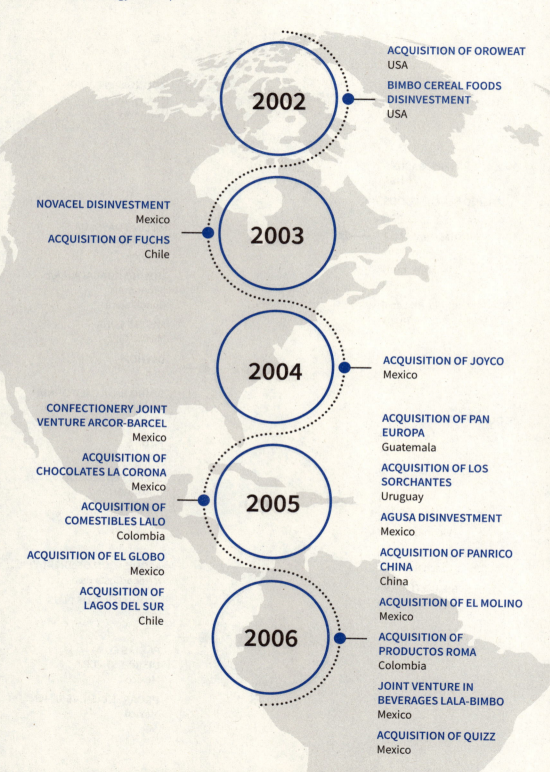

Chronology of plants 205

2007

ACQUISITION OF LA FAVORITA
Panama

ACQUISITION OF AGUA DE PIEDRA
Chile

ACQUISITION OF PAN CATALÁN
Uruguay

ACQUISITION OF ROLLY'S
Peru

2008

ACQUISITION OF FIRENZE
Brazil

ACQUISITION OF LIDO POZUELO
Honduras

ACQUISITION OF GALLETAS GABI
Mexico

ACQUISITION OF GALLETAS GABI
Brazil

ACQUISITION OF MODERNA
Panama

ACQUISITION OF MAESTRO CUBANO
Uruguay

ACQUISITION OF PANTODOS
Paraguay

ACQUISITION OF LAURA
Brazil

COOKIES JOINT VENTURE LA MODERNA-BIMBO
Mexico

2017

ACQUISITION OF EAST BALT BAKERIES
Italy, France, Switzerland, Ukraine, Russia, Turkey, South Africa, South Korea

ACQUISITION OF GRUPO ADGHAL
Morocco

2018

ACQUISITION OF MANKATTAN GROUP
China

ACQUISITION OF READY INDIA PRIVATE LIMITED
India

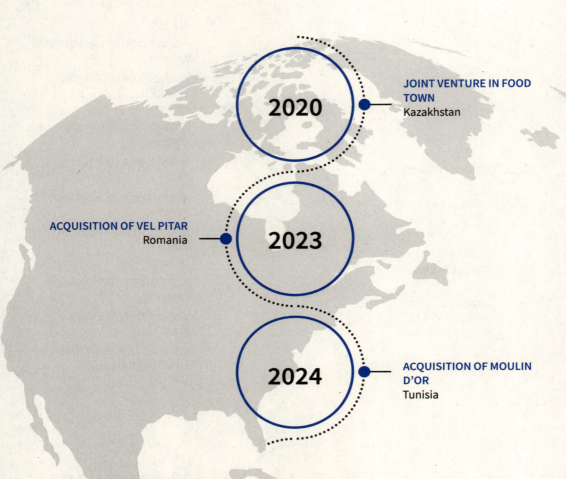

Appendix 2
Total quality and reengineering

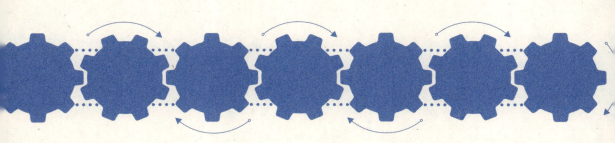

TOTAL QUALITY. A GENERAL PERSPECTIVE

First stage. Making contact

In March 1985, a seminar was held based on the ideas of Philip B. Crosby, the creator of the concept of *zero defects* and author of the book *Quality is Free*. Crosby designed a complete methodology for implementing a Total Quality process consisting of 14 Steps, which was the seminar's core.

The meeting aimed to raise awareness of the importance of quality. This issue involves everyone and must be constantly improved for a company to remain successful in the market.

The seminar had a significant impact, so a new position, the Head of Total Quality, was created in all the Organization's bakeries to promote this process. At the same time, a Corporate Total Quality Director was appointed to coordinate the project throughout the Group.

In some bakeries, Quality Improvement Committees (the first of the 14 steps) were set up to oversee planning, organizing, and directing the process. Plans, forms of progress control, problem analysis meetings, etc., began to emerge, and an awakening of the Company towards comprehensive improvement began.

The beginning of change

By the end of 1985, in the first National Assembly of Total Quality Leaders, the difficulty of initiating and managing a change process of this nature began to crop up.

No one denied the importance of improving the quality of products and services; no one openly opposed the objectives of Total Quality. The disagreement lay in how it should be done, specifically regarding methodology, time, and resources. It was clear that the path to Total Quality was a difficult one and that once it was undertaken, it could not be abandoned; that it was not a fad, but rather a way of managing the Company, a gradual process of implementation of new attitudes and new systems which required constant support and a lot of patience.

Besides, the concepts were not radically new: *the cost of not doing things right, customer service, quality control,* and *the habit of improvement;* in one way or another, all of these had been considered in the context of our Bimbo Way. Therefore, Total Quality constituted, to a large extent, a reencounter with the organization's fundamental beliefs.

In fact, on December 2, 1945, as part of the announcement of the inauguration of Panificación Bimbo, we published that the Company desired *to serve with quality*. Why, then, was Roberto Servitje, one of our own, speaking of a turning point when giving the starting signal for the Quality process 40 years later?

The Company was in for a change in culture, greater flexibility and agility, and stepping away from the traditional way of doing things and avoiding doing them out of inertia.

Second stage

By the end of 1985, the Total Quality Corporate Department, led by Pablo Elizondo, began studying and assimilating the ideas of W. Edwards Deming, Joseph Juran and Kaoru Ishikawa, among other experts, and upon their implementation, the scope of possibilities to continue the process of change widened.

Corporate projects

Another new idea, Juran's notion that *improvement is only achieved through projects followed by more projects*, has shed the brightest light on continuing the Total Quality process. Given the need to achieve success, we decided to work on the five improvement projects in the Company, which are explained below.

1. *Staff turnover decreased throughout the Organization*. A Corrective Actions Team was created and comprised of personnel from the bakeries and corporate offices. This team conducted serious and in-depth research on the causes of such high staff turnover. The team's members traveled to all the bakeries to teach a seminar on the subject. Other teams of this type were also formed in the bakeries where this problem was most critical.

2. *Training improvement.* Bimbo has always attached great importance to this activity to achieve results and uplift associates. Based on this, specific seminars were held to analyze the company's training guidelines (from which training plans were derived in every department) listed below:

- To detect education and training needs.
- To motivate the staff's development.
- To make the leader directly responsible for the development of his staff.
- To train and educate, preferably at work.
- To ensure that no one occupies a position without being trained for it.
- To educate and train for self-control.

3. *Improvement of product freshness in the market.* Freshness is one of the pillars of success at Bimbo. Therefore, we must achieve the shortest possible time between product production and placement on the retail shelf. Hence, production shifts and the warehouse and dispatch personnel schedule were modified; transportation departure times were adapted, truck stock was eliminated, and optimization was implemented. Managing codes for picking up products and transport repair schedules were also adjusted.

4. *Implementation of an effective system at customs.* Regarding improving product quality, the importance of having raw materials that meet the established specifications arose.

The Customs Corporate Committee was established, and this team created a customs plan encompassing the main raw materials. The plan was successful: laboratories and their equipment were improved, more efficient raw material reception and storage systems were implemented, and a stricter position, which simultaneously guided suppliers, was adopted. Different, more rigorous tests for raw materials were established and supplemented, and their specifications were defined more precisely. This procedure was improved as more reliable suppliers were obtained.

5. *Standardization of product quality for exportation.* When Bimbo first considered introducing its products to the US market, serious problems related to the lack of standardization and adherence to the Food and Drug Administration (FDA) specifications emerged. This situation generated a corporate project that included activities specific to quality control so that export products met the strict requirements for selling abroad.

Later, this project expanded to become Product Quality, evolving to have deeper and more encompassing implications than in the beginning. The new project would drive the idea that *we will manufacture all our products as if they were destined for exportation—and even better*.

One of the fundamental concepts learned at this stage was that 85 percent of change is in the hands of management, which owns the systems.

That meant that people wanted to do things right. In fact, people almost always want to do things right. When they don't, it is because their leaders did not specify what they expected of them, they do not know how to do so or they lack training.

Third stage. Support aspects

Several measures were implemented during this stage to contribute to the proposed change. Below is a list and explanation of these measures.

1. *Corrective Actions Team* (EAC for its Spanish acronym). Of the 14 steps in Crosby's program, one of the first explicitly mentions creating a Quality Improvement Committee to guide and bring about change. These committees evolved to become Corrective Actions Teams. This type of team is a hybrid that, as it meets the statistical segment in the Quality Circles, is operated in an interdisciplinary manner with the participation of leaders, associates and even members of different departments.

The EACs were widely used, established in almost all bakeries, and had different measures of success. Those who adhered to the methodology and faced specific problems obtained positive results.

2. *The obvious ones.* Another relevant process for implementation that stemmed from the Technical Area headed by Arquímedes Celis, back then coordinator of the production departments in the bakeries, was the emphasis on solving obvious problems that were evident and easily identifiable. For example, order and cleanliness, poorly calibrated equipment, a lack of training of associates, a lack of adherence to formulas and methods, etc.

3. *The concept of assurance.* At that stage, the concept of Quality Assurance also began to be applied, based on slightly more technical and production-oriented factors, implying the need to create a culture of self-control and prevention throughout the process.

In many of our operations, we can still see Process Letters, which encompass some factors that must be controlled to achieve the quality desired characteristics in our products.

Also, in combination with statistical learning, quality assurance influenced the need for statistical process control (SPC).

The three main items in this stage were the Total Quality Management concepts seminar, the Seven Basic Tools workshop, and finally, the Quality Assurance seminar, which was taught on multiple occasions. Handbooks, manuals, and didactic materials were created for this purpose, with exercises and practical cases from the Company.

Fourth stage. Consolidation

A model emerged for implementing quality management from a seminar taught to top management to subsequent meetings. The essential characteristic is that the model was our own; that is, it was generated by and for Grupo Bimbo and was based on three main principles:

- customer centricity;
- teamwork;
- process administration.

Bimbo quality model

The Bimbo Model consists of the following four phases:

Phase I. Preparation to start. In this phase, many actions were carried out, all aimed at achieving awareness, understanding, commitment and leadership for continuous improvement. In this phase, the following stand out:

a) Generating a mission.
b) Working to create the right atmosphere.
c) Generating policies.

Phase II. Understanding the processes and projects kick-off.

Definition of processes
The first effort to define processes can be concretely reflected in the compilation of each functional department. The processes related to the area have been properly documented. In this sense, the next step is for each team to have the relevant processes they must manage (identifying, defining, measuring, controlling, and improving them).

Upon defining the processes of different areas, the need to identify the main processes of the Organization was detected. Hence, the term *macro process* was born, and the process of identifying their functioning began.

However, in addition to the need to define macro processes, the possibility of modifying them to reflect the best business practices worldwide and make the Group more competitive was considered.

Then, the concept of Reengineering and the ten macroprocesses emerged.

Upon conceiving Reengineering as the process of *reinvention of processes,* there was confusion regarding its connection to the Quality process. It was thought that Reengineering was designed to replace Quality, which would no longer be Quality but Reengineering. The development of Reengineering in Grupo Bimbo is also used as a strategy to seek greater competitiveness. It is important to mention that when we understood the processes (*Phase II*), we realized that we even had to question their *zero-based* nature; that is, not to try to improve something that did not require it.

Starting the projects
Intense work was conducted in the different operations of the Group to conclude at least one project per department successfully. In each bakery, these projects had to have specific characteristics:

1. Focus on improving productivity rates and supporting the goals of each department.
2. Be executed with strict adherence to the quality methodology.
3. Contribute significant and transcendent profits for the Group's operation.

In addition to the economic benefits obtained, it is important to highlight that the work teams' use of a methodology to solve real problems that arose daily in their area has generated a culture of improvement in all participants.

Phase III. Processes and projects control.

Phase IV. Continuous Improvement.

Total quality and reengineering 217

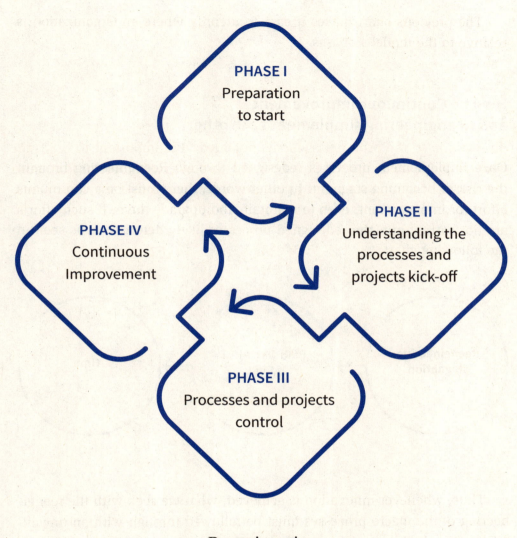

Reengineering

The previous chart makes it easy to identify where an Organization is relative to the model's phases.

How do Continuous Improvement and Reengineering supplement each other?

Once implemented, processes redesigned through Reengineering brought the risk of becoming stagnant. In other words, there must be a continuous effort for improvement, even to maintain and upgrade them. If such efforts are not carried out, the redesigned processes likely deteriorate, as seen in the following chart.

Thus, whenever innovation is achieved, what we seek with the reengineering of the macro processes must be followed through with an unwavering effort for constant improvement. This is part of the cultural change Grupo Bimbo is pursuing.

Total quality and reengineering 219

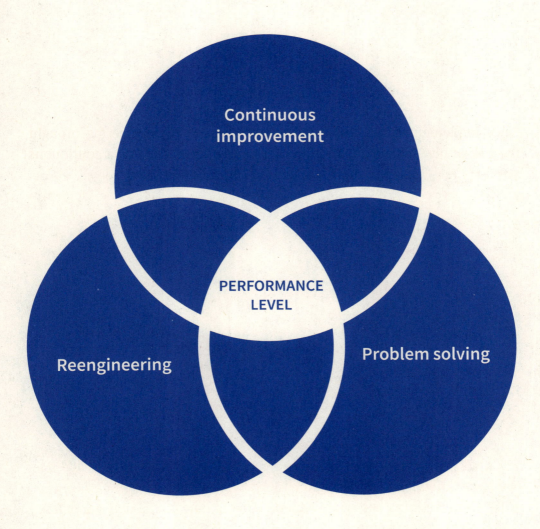

Epilogue

I would not want to end this book without insisting on something that I consider essential to ensure the success of any company.

I have addressed this several times throughout this book, but I feel it necessary to express it more clearly.

I am talking about the importance of decision-makers, such as entrepreneurs, directors, and managers.

We have reiterated, *"The company is what its people are, and its people will be what their managers are."* This is a massive truth, which is why it is crucial that these leaders, managers or entrepreneurs be true leaders who meet the requirements we have discussed.

The company will be excellent, good, or mediocre, depending on what its leaders are. Outstanding leaders are not those who stand out the most but rather those who have values, knowledge, discipline, and an unwavering will to serve well.

I conclude by saying that a company's success will depend on its ability to discover and support valuable people and its capacity to dismiss, with all necessary kindness, those who do not achieve that excellence.

Roberto Servitje

Final note

I have been asked more than once what my ideology is: rightist, leftist, or center. I always respond that my ideology is to respect people's dignity, responsible freedom, life, and family, social justice, reducing inequality, practicing a market economy with social responsibility, and human rights and the common good. I also favor democracy, the Welfare State, public order, national unity and peace.

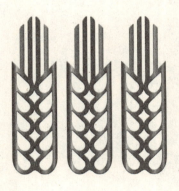

This work was printed
in the month of February, 2025,
in Impregráfica Digital, S.A. de C.V.,
Av. Coyoacán 100−D, Col. Del Valle Norte,
C.P. 03103, Benito Juárez, Ciudad de México.